THE
FRACTURED
FAMILY

By LEONTINE YOUNG

Out of Wedlock
Wednesday's Children
Life among the Giants
The Fractured Family

THE FRAC-TURED FAMILY

LEONTINE YOUNG

McGraw-Hill Book Company

New York • St. Louis • San Francisco • Düsseldorf
Mexico • Montreal • Panama • São Paulo • Toronto

First McGraw-Hill Paperback Edition, 1974

1 2 3 4 5 6 7 8 9 MU MU 7 9 8 7 6 5 4

Library of Congress Cataloging in Publication Data

Young, Leontine R
  The fractured family.
    1. Family—United States. I. Title.
HQ536.Y68   301.42'1'0973   73-2738
ISBN 0-07-072377-X

To my grandmother, who taught me how wonderful a grandmother can be

Contents

Acknowledgments

It is impossible to list all the people who talked with me in groups and individually about the realities of family life as they experienced it. I am deeply grateful to all of them for their willingness to give time and to share their thoughts and feelings. My gratitude goes to those persons who made the meetings possible. My special thanks to Grace and Sidney Reiss for their help and unstinting encouragement.

Introduction

This started out to be a book about grandparents. The subject seemed logical enough. There are many thousands of grandparents all over the country, and while they have received some attention as what are euphemistically known as "senior citizens"—though plenty of them aren't senior by any standard—they haven't been given much thought as grandparents. That role, in fact, seems to have faded into a misty, formless ambiguity. Grandparents are nice to have around, but at the same time they may easily become a problem.

Grandmothers are with cheerful inconsistency regarded as sweet old ladies who spread love and conflict in about equal proportions and as svelte, modern women who look fantastically young and engage in fantastic new ventures, usually successful. People are either amazed at what they can do or uneasy at what they may do, depending on the direction of their activities. There is a general feeling that where their grandchildren are concerned they may engender any number of conflicts, but in the community they are seen as a force for good, if not progress. Grandfathers are not usually seen as either sweet or dangerous. They are either successful or retired, too busy or in need of "something to do." As grandfathers they don't have much of a public image.

This situation is much stranger than the focus of our attention would indicate. We worry endlessly about parents and children, but once the children have in their turn become parents, the spotlight moves decisively. The original pair is left to grope their way into a new spot or recede gracefully into the shadows; for better or worse their work is done. There are, to be sure, a few bright, fleeting pictures: grandmother happily welcoming a new baby, grandfather escorting a small boy through the zoo—but these pictures have something of the quality of slides of the family vacation: they have little to do with every-day life. Grandparents have that indefinable aura of the visitor.

The abruptness of this transition has gone largely unobserved. It is taken for granted, like a fact of nature. As parents people are center stage; as grandparents they are pushed into the wings and ignored. Parents (or at least mothers) talk a great deal about the importance of being people as well as parents, about their need for individual self-expression. Grandparents don't have to talk about such things. They are only intermittently considered as anything but people, and they're *expected* to discover modes of individual self-expression. What they think about all this is not a question deeply explored, and in our youth-glorifying culture the tacit presumption is that it may not be worth exploring, even by the grandparents themselves.

So I began talking to groups of grandparents. But I also talked to groups of parents and to young adults not yet married. Through local organizations such as churches, women's groups, boards of social agencies, educational groups such as the sociology department of a college or, in one case, a kindergarten association—wherever I could secure personal contacts—I asked for small groups to meet with me. I made only one stipulation: so far as possible the people should be representative of our solid, back-bone population that seems to have no special or unique problems, people who have benefited from our society or who appear generally satisfied, except as their way of life is threatened by those not so satisfied.

The groups I met with were small, varying in numbers from four to sixteen. The people weren't related to one another, so there seemed to be no reason on that score for personal reticences or reservations. They were all middle-class, well-dressed, well-mannered, mostly well-educated. They appeared financially comfortable, moderately conservative, generally thoughtful. Even the young people were on the mild side, which doesn't mean they were oblivious to the defects of the system but rather that they seemed to feel no overpowering urge to take it apart. The people of all three generations conveyed a feeling of stability, a quality that has characterized the middle class and has seemed to guarantee its continuity through any succession of alarms and calamities.

I didn't ask many questions. I wanted to know what these people saw as questions, what they would spontaneously consider of first importance. I was not, after all, making a study with proper sampling procedures and carefully tabulated results. I wanted the *human* story: what people were thinking and feeling about their own family experiences, about what had happened to them in this confusing, changing era. After an initial few moments of uneasy self-consciousness while people tried to determine what I wanted, they concluded correctly that I didn't know either, and proceeded to discuss what they were interested in.

One surprising result, at least to me, was how similar the discussions were. I talked with groups from the suburbs of New York, from a small town in Michigan, from the plains of Illinois, from a midwestern urban area, from a small city in North Carolina, from another in Mississippi, from a big city and a small one in the Northwest. Everyone spontaneously talked about the same concerns with much the same attitudes, described the same questions and problems, followed the same patterns of meeting (if not solving) them. Only in one small religious community was there a marked difference, and even here the world was crowding in and the fears had a familiar ring.

The differences among the groups were generational, not regional. Yet even these differences were more a matter of perspective and manners than of radically different questions and approaches. The grandparents were more reserved, less adept at expressing their own ideas and feelings. They had never quite conquered the prohibition of their youth that one does not discuss family matters in public. Their true feelings appeared obliquely in casual remarks that everyone in the group appeared to take for granted. The grandparents had none of the lust for self-revelation that is so commonplace now; in fact they had a certain wariness of words that could not be smoothly attached to subjects safely separate from themselves. Not that they were afraid, certainly not in any obvious sense; but the whole idea was alien to them, and they tried the temperature of discussion as if they were dipping their toes in the ocean too early in the season.

The parents, on the other hand, slipped without effort into the well-practiced groove of talking about family problems. The difficulty was that they were accustomed to talking about themselves and their children, not about themselves and their parents. Their own childhoods and their feelings about their parents rarely obtruded, giving one the impression that either the subject was irrelevant for them or that they preferred not to think about it. There were exceptions, people who talked with deep interest and feeling about their parents and their past, but they were unusual. Most parents talked about the present and the future with grim tenacity, as if life were an obstacle race that must be run. They might have trouble with the subject, but they had no trouble talking. Discussions were the coin of the day, and words an accepted vehicle of self-expression.

The young of course had no trouble. They too had grown up in a talking age, and they enjoyed it. They talked about grandparents rather more than parents, and they were often more favorably inclined to their grandparents than to their parents—a phenomenon probably not confined to this generation. What was surprising was that they talked more about family as such than did either the parents or grandparents, and they were talking about something they had missed. For some it was family rituals like turkey dinner at home on Thanksgiving, for others it was relatives living close by and filling the house with noise and security, for still others the continuity of neighborhood and house and familiar routines. For all there was a wistful longing for something they could not name, a feeling of something important missed but still only vaguely sensed and symbolized by family as an ideal, an inchoate dream.

These were not young people in trouble. Nor were they, as far as one could see, alienated from their own families. They were thoughtful, well-educated, alert to the surges and conflicts of the day. Yet they seemed more aware than their parents or grandparents that some deeply important quality had gone out of the family, and they felt a loneliness for it. Even when some of them remarked casually, "Of course the family is falling apart," they referred obliquely to this feeling.

All three generations shared a sharp interest in the subject. They were under no pressure to participate in the groups, but they came, often at considerable personal inconvenience. And they stayed. Once involved they talked for two and three hours. Some called back later to say they had gone home to continue their exploration of what family meant to them, that they had not realized how they really felt. The parents particularly seemed to be opening new perspectives for themselves. Some observed that they had never before talked or thought about family as such. They were used to family problems, but these had always seemed to be more or less individual matters. Family as a force in the lives of everyone had been like the weather—something that was always there.

As might be expected, there were usually more women than men in the groups. The men who did come, particularly the young men, displayed little of the "the family is woman's business" attitude. They were not embarrassed or uncomfortable in their concern for family, children, human relations; they were not even cautious in displaying strong emotions on the subject. Whether this was the result of an impromptu process of self-selection or a signal of a changing pattern I would not know. Whatever the reason, there were only traces of that curious delineation of sex roles that has decreed family emotions and relationships are a feminine preserve. Grandfathers might be less confident than grandmothers, but their grandsons were not.

What the groups made abundantly clear, of course,

was that the grandparents of today could not be understood outside the context of changes in the family as a whole—and that is why I reached the decision to broaden the scope of this book to include all three generations. All three were caught up in those changes, and were talking about how they had been affected and how they reacted. They were talking, in fact, about what had happened to family as a structure and way of life in the short span of a few years. The past had slipped away almost under their eyes, and now seemed as ancient as a knight in armor; the future was shrouded in confusion: the present was laced with turmoil and anxiety. Yet the people of each generation with that marvelous human capacity to adapt were seeking new certainties, new means of meeting ancient needs.

They did not set out to analyze the changes. Living in the midst of them, they could not reach for the comforting perspectives of time and distance. Without being aware of it they were impressive in the tenacity of their struggle, in the courage and cheerfulness of their efforts. As they repeatedly observed, they were the fortunate ones. Quite possibly they were.

The first half of this book described the recurring themes that emerged from our discussions. Certain reactions and concerns appeared over and over again. The language might vary and the judgments reflect the individual, but the impact of the situation elicited attitudes and responses spontaneously selected and essentially alike. While I have included my own attitudes and judgments, I have attempted to describe how each generation regarded the themes that form a thread through their discussions. Each generation saw them from the context of its own interests and obligations, but to a surprising extent each was concerned with them.

The second half of the book is an attempt to put what these people said into the perspective of time and place. Their perceptions have much to say about family as family, about what great and rapid technological and social change has done to our personal lives, about the old and new problems that confront us. These people were acutely aware of change, but almost as an overwhelming, undifferentiated abstraction, and their attitudes toward it were ambivalent and uncertain. I hope that the very attempt to identify the changes that have so drastically influenced family structure and strength may help us understand a little better what we are all living and experiencing today.

1

PEOPLE WITH
A PAST

People over fifty—and contrary to the popular impression, there are quite a number of us—share a common experience. We have a past. Dull or exciting, fruitful or sterile, happy or miserable, we have a past. We also share a stubborn belief—important to us if not to society at large—that our memories, encapsulating all we have learned from life, are important to society. We don't dare say so because we are constantly being told that we are irrelevant, that nothing much we learned before 1960 matters to anyone. There has been, we are informed, an irreparable break with the past, and experience is merely another casualty of the space age. If the sheer volume of such disparagement doesn't intimidate us, the technological miracles must. Can we really believe that the small victories and defeats of a life, its inevitable compromises and disappointments, matter before the miracle precision of the computer?

But nobody with a spark of self-respect willingly submits to being filed away on a back shelf like an outdated textbook, and nobody with a sliver of insight really believes that technology always supersedes human experience. Still, this is an age when the old certainties that like compass points helped you know where you were and where you were heading are being swept into confusion. We over-fifties have memories; they are part of us, and a part of a process, of a continuity that stretches back over the history of many lives, centuries of lives. Nobody can disown those memories without disowning himself, but to concede that one no longer matters to his own society, any more than a worn-out tire, is self-obliteration.

It's a pretty problem—and a phony one. Human experience is never irrelevant, and it lives on despite all the noisy attempts to bury it in the ashes of the past. The grandparents I talked with in preparing this book for the most part were still doing what they had been doing all their lives: adapting to the demands of survival. Obviously they had done a pretty good job, but it's doubtful that they thought much about it. They were too involved in the process—and anyway, nobody rolls out brass bands for survival.

These grandparents talked about the present, not the past. If they had complaints, they kept them to themselves. They knew that one has to be involved, busy, interested in community affairs, independent, and, above all, adaptable. They had no criticism of younger generations—either their children's or their grandchildren's—or, if they did, they didn't voice it. They were, in fact, much too agreeable. There were exceptions—people who emerged in sharp outline as individuals—but most of these serious, hard-working, decent people had taken on the protective coloring of neutrality, a smooth surface blandness that in a group at least reflected exteriors rather than revealing an interior.

The over-fifties, like everyone else, have paid a price for that necessary adaptability. It's not that they mind living in the present—people have always had to do that to survive. But their present is so often cut off from the past that their past is discredited. Who wants to hear about what life was like forty years ago? What is of concern now is what life will be like forty years from now. Who bothers to relate the two? Then, too, so many people have been uprooted that there is no one to share common memories with, to make them important, to bring them perspective as part of the life process. And so these people are separated from a part of themselves, left in a queer half-world, without the strong emotions that attach to strong ties. Such ties have their roots deep in the past, and they have been eroding for a long time.

Yet people don't really have to stay in that half-world. With a little confidence they can refuse to be classified as irrelevant—or to be classified at all. People don't stop being people on their fiftieth birthdays—or, for that matter, on their sixtieth, seventieth, or eightieth. Underneath the bland surface, underneath the uncertainty and anxiety, an individual person lives on; and whoever and whatever he is, age is likely to make him more so. In a sense we are all brainwashed by our penchant for sweeping classifications.

We insist upon talking about "the old" and "the young" and relating any ideas we don't like to either "the past" or "the modern day." With a monolithic simplification we assume that a location in time provides a foolproof classification system, and even justifies whatever follies we are at the moment indulging in. There is a lot of comfort in blaming everything we find obnoxious on "the times." Since no one knows what to do about "the times" anyway, we might just as well relax and bemoan their less desirable aspects in comfort. It is such a tidy solution, so neatly packaged and so happily divorced from personal responsibility.

Unfortunately, people as people—which is to say, as individuals—aren't very tidy. They come in all sizes and shapes, and they aren't even very consistent. They are, as they've always been, bright and stupid, pleasant and unpleasant, peaceful and belligerent, generous and stingy, and heir to all the complexities and contradictions and ambiguities that have for a very long time characterized the human animal.

This is not to say that society hasn't changed. For it obviously has. Older people are more acutely aware of that than most of the young. They've lived through the changes, and have had to make what adjustments they could. Some of the adjustments have been truly admirable; and people have grown in understanding, in consciousness of themselves and their relation to their world, and in their ability to contribute to it. Others have found it simpler to adjust to modern conveniences than to modern thinking and have settled for fighting a rearguard action against all new ideas while, with oblivious inconsistency, they enjoy all the new advantages. A few have simply given up and retreated. But on the whole the older generations have managed to stay afloat in a period of unprecedented change.

That is a basic reality that all of us over-fifties should regard with respect and even some justifiable pride. It's taken quite a bit of doing. Change has always been something people preferred to take in small doses, and for some time now we've been forced to swallow a lot of it much faster than we've been able to digest it. Still, a good many people have managed to raise families, fulfill obligations, hang on to a few stray values, and even be reasonably constructive citizens. There are, in fact, older people who have managed to incorporate new perspectives, new ideas, new assumptions with their life-tested knowledge from the past and to evolve a coherent, enriched philosophy of living. That is a process a young person can emulate only with time—and with time he stops being young.

Older people are entitled to some respect from society—from its youthful members and from themselves—because they have survived and have developed enough flexibility to live with radically different problems and attitudes. They may or may not like the changes, but they live with them. Of course, some older people are easier to respect than others, but that's true of people at every age. The premise popular among some young people, and some not so young, that older people must *earn* the respect of those succeeding them overlooks the fact that they've *already* earned at least the first down payment.

That doesn't mean they're always right, and it doesn't mean they're always wrong, either. There really isn't anything very new about the recognition that age and wisdom are not necessarily synonymous: the observant young of every generation have noticed that. There has never been a shortage of foolishness at any age, as is borne out by our current obsession with classifying people by age and attributing a complete set of attitudes, ideas, and behavior to them as a consequence.

There are older people who, like a train engine, can only move on tracks. They may go forward or back, but their capacity to maneuver is nearly nonexistent. They cling less to the values of the past than to its myths and manners. Their hatred of the young is a measure of their own fear and disillusionment and, perhaps, their own long-buried dreams and longings. They can always be recognized by the even-handed monotony of their responses. They don't seem to have any priorities in the scale of their belligerence. A boy's long hair elicits much the same horror as an impassioned defense of a hypothetical revolution. The fact that the founding fathers had long hair and participated in revolution is an irony that escapes them.

There are also older people who do listen to new ideas, and come to realize that some of the teachings of their own youth are wrong and always were wrong. The pity is that they are not more listened to by people of every age. The capacity to change convictions and attitudes—the capacity for growth—is desperately needed always. It speaks, of course, with the voice of reason, and that is hard to hear at a time when volume of noise stands in for vigor of intelligence.

One of the disastrous consequences of a loss of confidence is a brand of creeping paranoia. Its symptoms have become common, and its advantages are obvious and persistent. There is a comfortable immunity from personal responsibility, a freedom to add to an ever-growing list of grievances, and a delightful dream of self-importance—since only importance could account for such a barrage of injustice. But the disease is contagious, and in time everyone ends up accusing and being accused by just about everyone else. And that leads to a lot of confusion.

The older generations can accuse the young of a long list of misdeeds, and in the resulting smog the unimportant gets mixed up with the important. More recent generations in reply accuse their elders of creating all the trouble in the first place. Everyone is so busy defending himself that there is no time to look at the problems. Now we're not only separated by a time classification, we're lined up behind the breastworks, glaring warily at each other over the top, ready to duck at the drop of a bottle.

By this time we're well into the next stage of the disease, the "all or nothing" syndrome. Once the battle lines are formed and manned we're in no mood to study pros and cons, let alone concede any good points to the enemy. The stage is set for the "non-negotiable demands" phase. While these words themselves are generally used by young radicals, the unyielding behavior they imply is common to all generations. The school principal who calls up the heavy artillery over a haircut can do little more for a riot. The college students—or, these days, their juniors in high school—who are ready to perish to the last man to share in an administrative committee can only perish all over again when they are pushed and shoved into those neat academic molds so dear to the heart of bureaucracy.

The trouble is that life isn't usually an all-or-nothing affair. There are only a few grievances worth all-out effort, and nobody has the energy for many of those anyway. Innocent simplifications are not very practical for dealing with the complexities of our day. Our problems are real; and old, not so old, young, and not so young are all a part of them. Each generation proceeds to view and judge them from its own vantage point—as generations have always done through the ages. So long as change was reasonably slow and deliberate, it didn't make for too much trouble, since vantage points tended to be pretty close together. If a son became a little tired of waiting for papa's power to wane, he implied no radical disagreement with the existence of that power. The generations long ago got used to the "move over and make room for me" problem, and people individually and collectively worked out their own ways of dealing with it. That's a very different situation from "get out of the way, your world is gone."

But with the rapid pace of change in our time, vantage

points have leaped apart. Even worse, in the general confusion no one can be sure where he is. What seems perfectly legitimate self-interest at one point can turn into a snare and a delusion in a remarkably short time. Older generations may be sure they want to maintain the status quo. But what status quo? The younger generations are pretty sure they don't want any status quo they've seen so far, but they are considerably less clear about what they do want. Perhaps the one consistent difference is that older people would like to slow the pace of change and younger people would like to speed it up. But even that depends a good bit on what is to be changed.

In the meantime every generation, except the very youngest and oldest, shares a good deal in common with every other. Each in its own language and its own way portrays confusion, anxiety, and a strange sense of helplessness. Each seeks solace within its own ranks and assumes it cannot be understood by any other. Each is a lot less sure of itself than its more vociferous protestations would lead one to believe. Most of all, each generation suffers a loneliness that is the product of its isolation and division.

Whatever the failures of the past, they will not be changed by denying the past, by cutting it off from the present. Santayana said, "He who refuses to remember the past is doomed to relive it." The older generations who have lived through so much have the greatest challenge of all: to find again their own past and to make it relevant to the present and the future. Youth may not be aware of it yet, but they're going to need that past, and their need will be great.

2

"OF COURSE, WE'RE
A VERY CLOSE FAMILY"

"Of course, we're a very close family." The words, spoken half-defiantly, as though the speaker expected some challenge, were often on the lips of grandparents, especially grandmothers. The specifics were always the same: children and grandchildren visited and were visited; there were regular holidays, vacations, presents, letters, telephone calls.

Parents with children still at home did not often speak about closeness. They talked about the rat race, the never-ending demands, their worry for and about their children. They spoke uneasily about their own parents, and then they too talked about visits and holidays and letters and telephone calls. Some said openly that they felt guilty because they didn't have more time for their parents, and they were openly relieved when so many others shared the same unease. Some were anxious and worried because parents were alone or far away or ill. Only a few spoke about these matters with relaxed comfort and assurance.

They were all talking about distance—geographical distance. People moved and moved and moved again, and family members scattered over thousands of miles. No one questioned the pattern; like the weather, it was there to be adjusted to, either happily or resentfully. You moved to take a better job or because the company transferred you or because the climate was better. Now and then someone moved because of people.

An attractive woman in her early sixties spoke with bitter helplessness. "When my husband died, I was alone. I wanted to be near my daughter, so I sold my home and moved to the town where she lived. I didn't know anyone there, but I took an apartment and I joined the church so that I'd meet new people." Half-apologetically she added, "I didn't want to be a burden to my daughter, but I wanted to be near her and my grandchildren. I knew she was busy so I planned to find new activities for myself. It worked out pretty well. Only of course the children were so busy too that I didn't see as much of them as I had expected."

She patted her smartly coiled gray hair nervously. "But then my son-in-law was transferred to another state. I don't know what to do now. I can't keep following my daughter from state to state; it doesn't make sense. Besides, they will all be busy, meeting new people, making a place in a new community. But it doesn't make sense either to stay where I am. The people are nice, but I don't really know any of them very well. I suppose I could go back to the town where I lived before, but actually there isn't any reason for me to return." There was a flicker of panic in her eyes, although she looked so modern and competent, so well-groomed and smartly dressed, with that glaze of sophistication expensively bought.

Her story, with one variation or another, is so common as to be almost trite. The answer to her problems, we say, is simple. Make new friends, get interested in new activities, travel, involve yourself. There is no tragedy here. This woman has enough money for her own security. The world is full of things for her to do and full of people like herself, older people with time on their hands. They won't share her past nor she theirs, but they can share the present. And she can visit her family—there will be holidays, vacations, letters, phone calls.

No one questions our need to move. We've always been a restless people. We crossed an ocean, settled a continent, built a powerful nation. We move to find jobs, to take a better job, to enjoy the sun, to fulfill a dream, and now we move to escape the world we have created. We've accomplished many things by moving, but we've destroyed things, too. Not the least of what we've destroyed has been family closeness.

We took the family for granted. At first we took the family with us when we moved, its traditions, obligations, and permanence. Then, as we moved faster and faster, we began to drop off the excess baggage that slowed us down. The family grew smaller and the time spent together shorter. Now family is parents and children, and their years together have shrunk to less than two decades. A bright-eyed, energetic young woman says briskly, "I have four years to influence my son in the basic pattern of his life. I know those first years are the most important, and they're the only time I'll have him all to myself. Then he'll go to nursery school, and after that the school and his own activities will take most of his time. Whatever I want to teach him, I have to do now."

She wasn't particularly troubled by the prospect. It was her reality, and she expected to make the best of it. If anyone had asked her about family closeness, she probably would have been surprised. She had a happy marriage, and she loved her son. She was familiar with the modern concept that the amount of time people spend together matters less than the way they use the time they do have. It is the quality of their relationship that counts, rather than the quantity of closeness. There is truth in that notion, but there's a joker in it too. Relationships grow through shared experiences, and sharing takes time together. Time is no guarantee of closeness, but it is necessary for that intimate knowledge upon which all closeness depends.

There's always the possibility, of course, that people have all the family closeness they want. There's nothing wrong with visits and letters, and long-distance calls are good for the telephone business. The contact is transient, pretty well controllable, commits nobody to much more than he wants to take on, and has a general tendency to keep just about everyone on his best behavior. Even those inevitable relatives that bring a heartfelt groan can be accommodated when they live far enough away and don't visit too long. There's simply no point in arguments and conflicts when people aren't going to be together for more than a few days, and in any case no one can really afford them. There's no time to mend a rupture in the delicate web of family relationships, and long separations may nourish solitary fantasies of injury that everyday contact would dispel.

There is no question that there are real advantages to a system that confines family relationships—at least those relationships beyond what we aptly call the immediate family—to small, neat periods of communication. The old conflicts and feuds, the underlying resentments, the dominations and rebellions, the unwanted advice and interference are starved out and confined to the small circle of parents and children. Grandparents may still interfere now and then, and family irritations may sputter into flame, but the old intensity is gone.

For many grandparents, too, there is a new freedom. They may enjoy their grandchildren and know that their responsibility will be brief. Even when there is no great distance to impose separation, they know the cardinal sin in the modern family is to interfere. If they have no power, neither are they burdened. More than one grandmother is happy to see the children come and breathes a weary sigh of relief as they go.

Obviously people would never have moved so blithely, or accepted so matter-of-factly those casual uprootings from one side of the continent to the other, if there had not been advantages for them. What is only slowly becoming apparent is the full implication of our loss of family closeness.

Grandparents deny that it is gone, at least for them, perhaps because they still have some memory of its lingering strength, perhaps because the years have brought home the terror of its loss. Parents are too busy, too harassed, too pushed from every side to think much about it yet. For the young it is already a fantasy, sometimes a dream glimpsed from the past, sometimes a grinding need to find what they've never had.

A serious, bright young man, soon to be married, said, "When I have children, I'm going to spend time with them. We're going to be *friends*. When I was growing up, we had Thanksgiving dinner on Wednesday night because my parents went to a party on Thanksgiving Day. That's not going to happen in my home. We'll have a family dinner on Thanksgiving Day and we'll have a turkey and every member of the family will be there." He spoke with bitter emphasis.

A naïve eighteen-year-old said wistfully, "The Depression must have been wonderful. I've heard my parents talk about it, and everyone was together; the whole family was in one place." She had never known physical want, but she had surely known a loneliness of soul.

One youngster told her mother, "I wish we had more relatives close by. It would be so nice to have a big family to walk down the street with, to do things with."

And then there are all the young people seeking with each other the family closeness that slipped away before they could know what it was. They live together, sharing what they have and seeking to present a united front to an outside world indifferent to their needs. There must be much that is fantasy in these ersatz families, whose members talk so bravely of love and peace and generosity and understanding. They speak the dreams people have dreamed over the centuries—only in the past people rarely tied them to the family. Whatever else the family has been, it has always been a thoroughly practical institution. It could never have survived the wear and tear of the centuries if that had not been so. Utopias have come and gone, but the family has plugged relentlessly on with its ceaseless business of ensuring the survival of the human species. It really has never been a romantic organization, and it's doubtful that any attempts to make it so have much of a future.

But the need for closeness is real, though we have lost the awareness of what it really meant. The family was dedicated to permanence, insofar as that is possible in an uncertain world, and permanence meant continuity. People belonged to a family, with lifetime membership. That meant security, a kind of security we have almost forgotten. Belonging for us is a sometime thing; we have either to earn it or win it or buy it, and even if we achieve it, there's no assurance we're going to keep it. We can't even imagine any more the kind of security that could be taken for granted, that was our right. And where could we find it now anyway? The family is too weak, too small, too temporary. We've even learned to exploit its weaknesses. Some parents dangle the loss of their love and care like a sword of Damocles over their children's heads to ensure the desired behavior; and others fear to cross their children, to demand or deny too firmly, lest they lose their children's love. Only a family that has forgotten the meaning of security could be prey to such fears.

This is a human tragedy, the tragedy of a terrible uncertainty, of a loss of confidence so great that no one, not even oneself, can be trusted. There is no place to go for the surcease that says here we belong, here we may take for granted and be taken for granted. The very idea is alien, if not, indeed, a blow to our *amour-propre*. In our world that spells a loss, not a gain.

We've forgotten the closeness that was the quiet growth of familiarity. In fact, familiarity is a little suspect these days. It smacks of dullness, of a failure to keep up. We not only prize new gadgets, we go hunting through cracks and crannies for new ideas. We even devote time and energy to devising ways of creating "new me's" and "new you's," preferably via some simple new method. No, familiarity doesn't seem to fit; yet closeness in human relationships of any kind is rooted in familiarity.

Closeness is most essentially mutual knowledge learned in the shifting kaleidoscope of living. It is the thousands of small pieces of daily experience: family laughter at a family joke, struggle among conflicting desires and needs, reluctant accommodations and compromise, quiet moments of peace enriching the web of routine, the splatter of irritation, shared grief. It is knowing what to expect of each other because each has lived through it all before. It is sharing in each other's lives. It is a process in time; and in the family where time was measured by the span of life, it was a process of shifting balances, of power surrendered and inherited, of change embedded in familiarity.

Because most people only dimly remember such closeness—and young people not at all—we nourish fantasies that somehow it was all synonymous with love and peace. In our conflict-riven world we dream of that Utopia as a starving man dreams of food. But mutual knowledge is not the same as mutual understanding, and family closeness offered security and belonging, not necessarily love and peace. It encompassed too many greedy and anxious egos for that. People were mainly concerned with keeping order and ensuring family survival, with mutual obligations and mutual protection. They enforced them with the weapons of custom, tradition, firmness of conviction, and unity of purpose.

It all seems as outdated now as a medieval knight in armor. Only it turns out that in our mad dash for the twenty-first century we not only shed the excess baggage, we lost some indispensables. And now we don't know how to find them again. We flock to sensitivity courses and spend our good money exposing our innermost thoughts and feelings to strangers. How could we know that the truly close family was one long training in sensitivity? Admittedly, people could and did use such knowledge and experience to hurt as well as to heal, to compete as well as to unite; but no course yet has come up with a way to dissolve human perversity or to assuage the strivings of the individual ego. At least the family accepted all that as part of living, and worked to set limits on the more excessive brands of its members' behavior.

Some of us now, in desperation, even seek instant intimacy. Touching, even the depersonalized touching of strangers, may open a way to feeling something real, to sharing an honest emotion with another. There were surely people who lived together all their lives who also knew the corrosive loneliness of inner isolation, but there must have been far fewer of them, and only the unluckiest could have found all paths closed. They were not naïve about emotions, because they felt them rather than talked about them. Even the more obtuse had to possess a pretty good working knowledge of human relationships, because in a truly close family there were no vacations from the relentless school of living. For better or worse, the insulation was pretty thin.

We've lost family closeness, but we haven't lost the needs it met. We've created a world where there isn't much place for those enduring, binding relationships, and suddenly we can't find our way in it.

3

PEOPLE VERSUS PROBLEMS

The grandparents, parents, and children I talked to all knew the family had changed, but then so had almost everything else in their world. The grandparents were most aware of change, because they remembered when the family had been different. Yet more than the other generations they seemed to accept change as though it were not only inevitable but had no personal impact upon themselves. They didn't say they were delighted with it or unhappy about it. Here and there someone did burst out with bitter denunciation, like the well-dressed man in his sixties who said, "I'll tell you about grandparents. They're the most neglected, the most useless, the most forgotten people in the country." Or some were unabashedly pleased, like the briskly efficient woman who remarked, "I have my own business and I'm doing well. I enjoy every minute of it. I'm glad to have my grandchildren visit for a couple of weeks in the summer, but to tell the truth I'm glad when they leave and I can go back to my office." But most had neither praise nor criticism. Family change existed, and there was nothing more to be said.

Such apathy may be the outward reflection of a deeply wounding culture shock. Certainly fear lurked behind the competence, the scheduled activities, the pleasure over the advantages of travel and new experiences and new acquaintances. There was something else too: a detachment from strong feeling about people, a blandness like cream sauce that seemed to cover the emotional flavor of the individual. It may have been only a protective covering, but it seemed more than that. Emotional investment, these people's attitude seemed to say, was too expensive, too dangerous. Separation is normal these days. Who can afford to care too deeply?

The parents, who remembered only a time when change had already altered the shape of family, were involved in the present. They talked about their children with great feeling, but without noticing they spoke mainly of problems. Outside conflicts and dangers threatened their influence on their children. They had no assurance of their own power to withstand those pressures, no assurance that their values would in turn become their children's values if the intrusive world beyond their doors so decided. They accepted that intrusiveness as an inevitable part of a changing social order to which they too could only submit. Worse, they had no assurance that what they did, what they believed, was right.

Over and over the questions were the same: "Did I do the right thing? Am I right to insist upon this? Was I wrong to let the children do that?" There was never an answer that brought the comfort of certainty or finality, and responsibility was a job without respite. No wonder more than one parent looked forward with longing to the day when his children would move out into the wider world and take with them for better or worse whatever they had learned, whatever they had become. The pain of separation was mixed now with relief from a responsibility that had carried too much worry, too much confusion. These were the conscientious parents, those who wanted for their children the happiness and satisfaction they felt should be their birthright. For them parenthood was an opportunity, but it was also a burden. Other parents fled from a responsibility that was too great and welcomed the intrusiveness of the outside world, shifting to its agents the work of bringing up their children. For them parenthood was *only* a burden; and their own failure belonged now to school, to community, to the system.

When these middle-aged people talked of their children, the words had tumbled out, crowding upon each other. But when they spoke of their own parents the feeling was sharply different; the words came slowly, sometimes haltingly, sometimes not at all. They were uneasy, often guilty, and nearly always perplexed. For their parents were a problem too.

How do you care for parents who live hundreds of miles away? How do you make them a part of a busy life in which they have no natural place, no predetermined purpose, no vital service to give? How do you meet the demands of children, work, and community along with the needs of parents growing older? How do you stretch yourself thin enough to reach both backward and forward and yet meet the impact of the present? How do you find breathing space for yourself? These questions brought anxiety and pressure, tension and guilt. Concern struggled in a climate already unfriendly to its growth. It was more burden than opportunity, more obligation than satisfaction.

Now and then there were those left free of problems, free to feel happiness and closeness between two generations. A young woman in a small Canadian city said wonderingly, "I wouldn't know what to do if I didn't have my mother close by. She lives just a couple of blocks away and we talk, if only for a few minutes, every day. Who else would share with such pleasure the small everyday things—my baby's first words, the day he first tried to stand? Who else could I turn to when I'm worried because he doesn't feel well? Of course I share these things with my husband, but he's gone all day, and in any case these are so often woman-to-woman things. My mother has had the experience with babies and children, and both my husband and I depend on her."

But another young mother said angrily, "I wish my mother-in-law would stop telling me what to do about my children. I want to do things my way, not hers. I wish we lived a long way from her and then I'd be free."

One of these young mothers welcomed what the other rejected, but both were personally involved and both had personal feeling. They were individuals reacting to their own individual circumstances, with vitality and familiarity. They still had room for the emotional range that constricts when people begin to merge into problems.

Youth normally is concerned with itself, and certainly the young people of our day have much to concern them. For them the present state of the family is normal because they remember no other. Separation is as inevitable as breathing. It occurs not when they are ready, not when they feel that burst of confidence that longs to test itself in the world, but at a specified date in time. When they finish high school, they are expected to move on. Ready or not, there it is. Young people seek from each other a security that they do not expect to find in family. They look not to parents or grandparents, sometimes because they are not sure they will find the understanding they seek, sometimes because they are not expected to seek understanding in another generation. Things aren't structured that way.

The young counsel the young. They help each other to make the momentous life decisions. They talk of concern for each other, of closeness and sharing of intimate thoughts and actions. Even here separation is always a hazard. One young man just graduated from college said, "A little over a year ago I took a job in New York because so many of my friends from college were there. We were going to stay together, to keep the ties we had formed to each other. Now there are only two of us left. The others have scattered to different cities. Soon, I suppose, one or both of us will be gone too. When we meet again, we may be strangers to each other. This is a very lonely kind of life. We're friends for a while, and then we're gone to meet new strangers that will become friends for a while."

The boundaries of a generation are shrinking to an ever-narrowing band. College seniors complain that they do not understand the entering freshmen. Or a college student revisits his old high school and stares aghast at those who have succeeded him. "We didn't behave like these kids; we didn't feel like these kids," he says uncomprehendingly.

For some young people, ties stretch back through the family from individual to individual. There was the college student who arrived to talk to me almost breathless, saying, "I shouldn't be here. I have a final tomorrow and I ought to be home studying. But I couldn't miss a chance to talk about my grandfather. He was really something. He lived with us when I was a little kid, and some of the best memories I have were the times we spent together. We went on walks, we worked together, and he taught me how to build things, how to whittle with a penknife. Sometimes we talked and sometimes we didn't. It didn't make any difference because we understood each other. We were friends. When I had worries, I took them to him. We shared things, and he could make the simplest everyday kind of thing fun and exciting—I guess because we shared it. He's been dead several years now, and I still miss him. I'll always remember what he taught me."

There were few young people with such an enduring strength of feeling. Strong emotions are the source of individuality in people. They define personality, and when they also have the strength of continuity, they color the whole structure of life. Here and there I talked to someone who remembered a grandmother, a father, a person who remained a vital spark in their lives, and they spoke in phrases that portrayed a personality:

"My grandfather was a patriarch with a long beard, and no child ever dared to pull it. . . ."

"My grandmother gave me something special, unworried love. . . ."

"My father told me that even though I was making good money as a computer programmer, he thought I was robbing myself of the experience with people that I really wanted. He was right, and I took a job teaching first grade at half the pay and twice the satisfaction. My father is a wise man."

This last was a Chinese woman who now cares for her

own three children and remarks matter-of-factly, "I don't mind my relatives or my husband's relatives interfering in my family. I don't have to follow their advice, but some of it is sound and helpful. And I respect them. How will my children learn to respect me if they don't see me respecting my parents?"

Few people expressed strong feelings about the family as such, or about individual family members. There was anxiety, concern, a kind of weary confusion, but the strong clear emotions were muffled—or perhaps they had never developed. It was difficult to realize in this emotional twilight that the family had once been the cradle of powerful emotions that gave color, vitality, individuality to people. The conflicts, rivalries, love and hate, loyalty and betrayal that were the stuff of great drama, tragedy and comedy, were strangely stilled. It was more than a lack of expression, for there was no sense that these emotions were there, or that people expected them to be there.

From *King Lear* to *Life with Father*, literature has found inspiration in the emotional intensity of family relationships. They shaped personality and gave significance to the individual even when his interests were subordinated to the family's. What he felt was important, if for no other reason than that he was an integral part of the total fabric.

But strong family relationships have gradually withered in a society that no longer nourishes them. People can't afford great emotional investment when separation is almost inevitable, when the pull of outside interests and pressures can fray with impunity through the vulnerable connections of human feeling and need. To be viable these days, family feelings have to be ready to take second place, to accommodate themselves to other concerns and greater urgencies. Individual family members have to develop outside resources to fill the vacuum, and find other means of meeting need. In the process, depth of feeling for a few tends to give way to shallow emotions more easily transplantable, more comfortably adapted to change and mobility. If part of individual personality—that added dimension of intense inner life—goes with the change, that too is noted less by its absence than by its consequence. Family structure changes, and the emotions that gave it life and power change with it.

Our society at large reflects the same apathy where the family is concerned. Everyone knows the family is in trouble. We read the divorce statistics, the lurid reports of wife-swapping, the accounts of neglected children, of drugs and vandalism and despair among the youth of the affluent middle class. We read about the forgotten old and the neglected young. We hear about the fathers who are too busy and the mothers, no longer needed, who seek escape from emptiness in alcohol or hectic activities and fruitless trivialities. We know about all this and accept it as an inevitable part of irresistible change.

Family problems become less and less those of domination, rivalry, competition. In their place grow emptiness, loneliness, anxiety, alienation. Family unity is subdivided not by conflict but by distance and diversity, and the segmentation of life batters at the cohesion of family and individual alike. The family as a way of life recedes from center stage to background, leaving in its wake a massive confusion and loss of confidence.

Grandparents, by their very silence, convey distrust of the value of any contribution they can make out of their own past. Parents, with their anxious question, "Did I do the right thing?" find no certainty within themselves. The young, better educated, better informed, more sophisticated than any generation before them, talk of identity and alienation and seek with restless energy for meaning and purpose. Self-doubt corrodes the very capacity for trust in another generation and leaves chasms of silence.

The violent feelings, anger, and disappointment break loose outside the family. Youth challenges as a group, attacking bitterly and sometimes with violence; and the reaction of its elders can be a terrible anger as well as hurt and bewilderment. Those who respond with such sweeping indictment also have children and grandchildren, and still they seem to see not individuals born into change, but aliens, a strange and dangerous species.

There can be few things more frightening and more shattering to basic confidence than the feeling that the generation coming to power is made up of people incomprehensible by any familiar standards, without islands of identification from a common past, from common human experience. It is not new knowledge, new technology, new modes of dress and speech, or even new philosophies and ideologies—it is the alienation of feelings, the emotional gulf that is so terrifying. When there are bonds of personal affection and loyalty, understanding can find a bridge; but when there is fear, hostility, or personal indifference, the gulf becomes unbridgeable. People become strangers and, with a regression to the primitive, the stranger becomes the enemy.

Some people, certainly, fight against this alienation. A busy, successful businessman took time to come and talk about his family because he was deeply and personally concerned. He lived in the same Southern city where he had been born and grew up. "I'm worried about what is going to happen to my children. I don't want them cut loose from family loyalties with no roots in their own past. I have six kids, and I live in a neighborhood that's full of children. My back yard is crowded with them most of the time. I know my children's friends and I know their parents.

"I like living in a city small enough so that I can get home quickly and keep in touch with a neighborhood. My parents and my wife's parents live here, and we see them every week. We plan it that way. I'm not going to have my mother and father feeling cut off from our lives, and I want my children to know their grandparents, to know they have a past. I don't want them to have the same ideas their grandparents had—or the same ones I have, for that matter. They live in a different time, and they have to think differently. I expect to have to run to keep up with them, and that's fine. That's the way it ought to be. But I don't want them turned loose without family loyalties and traditions." This father wanted his children rooted in the past, not buried in it.

A grandmother in central Illinois spoke of family responsibility—not of the requirement that her children care for her but of her responsibility to help her children and grandchildren. She was one of those sure of her own values, confident that the qualities creating meaningful human relationships had not and would not change. She saw responsibility as a creative endeavor, a satisfying self-discipline. "Responsibility to children," she said, "includes a lot more than physical care. It means setting expectations they can meet and leaving them inner space, inner freedom to grow." Like the father in the South, she was clinging not to an outworn past but to values and relationships that must renew themselves as long as people live together on a single planet. She was convinced that family values must not be lost in the maelstrom of change. She had a zest for life that grows rare amid our don't-get-involved attitudes. As she put it, "Life is to be used, not escaped."

One can see such people as the last of a dying breed; but that still leaves the question of why they are more alive, more exciting as people, more complete as individuals. Perhaps it is because they are more concerned with giving than taking, and they see personal responsibility and continuity of human relationships as opportunities, as personal fulfillment. They may indeed be the ones who offer hope for the future, a pattern of life that uses the best of the past to modify the present and build new faith in the future.

All of these people, of whatever generation, shared one thing. They were not divorced from their own feelings, and those feelings were rooted in the family. These people had a confidence in themselves that was a part of their life continuity. None of them wanted to return to the past; they were much too vital and realistic for that. Their concern was with the contributions of the past to the present and the future.

4

"THANK GOD, I'M NOT DEPENDENT ON MY CHILDREN"

Americans have a special feeling for independence. We began as a nation by declaring it, and we settled a continent with a multitude of personal declarations. Nowadays independence is enshrined in our pantheon of virtues as a law or a commandment.

So at first it didn't seem strange that the grandparents I talked to said so often, "Thank God, I'm not dependent on my children." They said it with such intensity and spontaneity that one might suppose dependence was one of life's more terrible misfortunes. That, indeed, is the way they felt about it—and that is strange. Independence is fine, but dependence is also a normal part of life. The family has been an organization with a long and honorable history in caring for dependents.

If people had said, "Thank God, I'm not dependent on the government," it would be more easily comprehensible. But they were talking about the family, and not just an individual family either. This was not the grandmother or grandfather alienated from their children by personal conflict and feud. In every group, in every part of the country, these steady, reliable, intelligent grandparents were saying the same thing: "Thank God, I'm not dependent on my children."

They had all worked to bring up their children, fed them, cared for them, educated them. They spoke of them with affection and pride. Not one complained that their children were ungrateful or were now refusing to help them. They were talking about something quite different, something that was not personal at all, though it had a drastic personal effect upon them. They were saying, "*I have no right* to be dependent on my children." I don't know whether they thought of it precisely that way, but that was the message they conveyed, and it was a message tense with feeling.

These people were also, by their very relief, implying that this escape from dependence was not to be taken for granted, lightly achieved, or easily won. There was an underlying uneasiness in their voices—after all, they had no guarantee that independence once won would remain. People grow older, less able to care for themselves, and these grandparents had reached an age where the fact of human mortality was a reality, not just an abstract possibility.

What were they talking about? Money? They were comfortable, and they did not give the impression of worrying too much about financial independence; besides, they had social security, pensions, and medical insurance, and many of them were working. They were not rich, but neither was financial disaster just around the corner. In fact, they were probably less worried about

money than people used to be, for there are more cush-
ions now, even if they are pretty skimpy ones, and
affluence becomes a way of life for older people as well as
for the young. Yet they never take affluence for granted in
quite the same way as the young. They remember the
Depression. They remember too, as one woman put it,
that "money rolls"—and it can roll away faster than it
was hauled in.

Still, these grandparents talked about trips and vacations and taxes and buying presents and houses and cars,
all the things that plague and delight the American
middle class. They certainly had their worries about
inflation, expensive illness, and the fluctuations of the
stock market; but these worries, in one form or another,
have always afflicted people. They didn't explain that
passion for independence.

Nor do they explain why parents, with the same
passion, said the same thing when they talked about the
future: "I never want to be dependent on my children."
In every group a parent would spontaneously raise the
issue, and the others nodded. No one said, "I don't want
my parents to be dependent on me." Maybe they felt that
way, but that isn't what they said. They weren't talking
about their parents when that wish burst forth; they were
talking about their children, and abruptly they were
talking about themselves. No one was saying, "I don't get
along with my son. I wouldn't want to be dependent on
him." That might be an individual tragedy, with other
parents replying, "I'm glad I don't feel that way." But
everyone understood this feeling, this dread of one
generation's dependence on another. Everyone understood that it had nothing to do with the individual parent,
the individual child.

What all these people were saying was that one

generation *should not* be dependent on the next one. And they were saying it as if it were a new commandment that must be obeyed if they were to remain members of society in good standing.

Actually, except by implication, no one talked about independence. They talked of their fear of dependence—a very different matter. Fear, like a fine red line, threaded its warning through the comforts and perquisites of the good life. If the older generation has no right to dependence on the younger, then such fear makes good sense. No amount of social security—which is at best economic, not social, and at worst not even economic—answers or can ever answer the intricate and interwoven needs of human beings. Beneath all the brave and cheery words is the knowledge that dependence is as much a part of life as independence. If the young fight to be free of the normal dependence of childhood, older people face the hazards of returning to it. Only now, people seemed to be saying, dependence could no longer be normal, because the links of interdependence were weakened and perhaps broken.

For many young people the dependence or independence of older people was naturally an abstract question, no part of their own experience. They took the necessity of independence for granted. A few talked of what the dependence of grandparents had meant to them personally. A grandparent living in their home had not usually meant a happy experience. One girl remarked with distaste, "I had to share a room with my grandmother when I was growing up. It was awful."

Another spoke with emphasis. "My grandmother grew up in Europe and now that she's alone she lives with us. She thinks we should behave just as she did when she was young. She's always interfering, always telling us what to do. My mother tries to stop her, to explain that things are different now, but that only causes arguments. My brother won't even speak to her half the time, and then she cries and feels hurt. I feel sorry for my mother. She's always in the middle." (Usually such complaints were about grandmothers, not grandfathers.)

Yet other young people spoke with deep feeling of the need of old people for their children. One girl not yet twenty talked indignantly of an old man taken ill in a summer hotel where she was working. His only child lived two thousand miles away. She called the son and told him about his father. After questioning her about the details, the son suggested, "Call me tomorrow and let me know how he is."

"What do you want me to do? Call and tell you he's dead?"

There was a startled silence. Then the son said, "You mean you think I should come now?"

"I certainly do," the girl answered.

The son was talking about his father's medical condition. The young woman was talking about his human need. As she explained indignantly, "What was wrong with that old man was loneliness. He could have died of it. When his son came he got better. I told the man that. He hadn't even thought about it. I told him he should take his father home to live with him. And he did."

In the past the family was built with the bricks of mutual need, each fitted to the other; and if they were not all a perfect fit, they were in the over-all structure strong and stable. Everyone is born helpless. And that's what parents are for—to take care of their young, to provide for their needs, to teach them what they must know to cope with the world, to protect them from its dangers while they are still too weak to protect themselves. In that there is no change. But today parents speak of an anxiety that would not have occurred to *their* grandparents: the danger of their needing their children in turn. One mother put it directly: "We have to be careful not to need our children too much. That would be unfair to them. It's natural for parents to need their children more than the children, once grown, need them. We have to plan ahead so that we will not be a burden to them. They have to be free of us."

She meant more than money, if indeed she was thinking of money at all. She meant the need to be a part of her children's lives, to keep them a part of hers. She meant the interdependence that gives each the right to depend on the other, not just in the crises of life but in the thousand small ways of everyday living. She was talking about the right to need her children as in their early years they had had the right to need her. Only now she was saying there could be no such right, because now her need would be a burden, a handicap to those who must travel far and fast.

For the grandparents of sixty or seventy years ago there was no such thought of burden. As children grew older, they were more able to manage for themselves. They married, set up their own homes, had children. They also expected their parents to remain a part of their lives; and the parents still felt some right to interfere in their lives, although they had lost the power of enforcement. Sometimes such interference made trouble, but everyone had family arguments. Sometimes it was a help, because experience was respected and had something to teach those who were still short of it. Sometimes, of course, a parent used his right to interfere in a way that robbed his children of their maturity, and he relied on a system that made that easy. But there were times when

each generation found in the right of interference comfort and strength, dignity in the shifting but unbroken
rhythm of time. As parents grew older, they relinquished
power and in turn became more dependent on their
children. Even then the need was not totally one-sided:
their children knew that they in turn would need the care
of their own children, that this was a transition in a
continuing process. As a Chinese woman still close to the
power of that process remarked, "If my children do not
see my respect for my parents, how will they learn to
respect and care for me when I am old?" The past, the
present, and the future flowed together, and since no one
expected great change no one really questioned the
rhythm of need and the meeting of need.

No grandparent or parent needs to be told that a world
like that is, in most places, almost as remote as the horse
and carriage. There are still pockets of timelessness, still
families where grandparents, or more likely a grandparent, live with their children and continuity is unbroken.
But the right to need and be needed is gone because the
system that made it work has changed. Now needs may
be continuing but they are only mutual for allotted spans
of time. The transitions have become breaks, and people
must adapt not to a way of life but to several ways of life,
each with a beginning and an ending. This is the day
when young mothers plan matter-of-factly to seek out
new interests, activities, and obligations while their
children are still in grammar school. No matter how
heavy the demands on their time, energy, and emotional
resources, they know they must have other outlets for the
fast-approaching years when their children will no longer need them. Otherwise they will be left with a vacuum
or will be tempted to burden their children with their
own need to be needed. Many will go to work—to help

send the children to college, or to find a place of their own in the active outside world. Their new life may be full or empty, exciting or dull, but almost certainly it will be less personal, less concerned with mutual need than it would in times past.

For fathers the breaks in time may be easier, at least until they reach the birthday that makes retirement mandatory. If life is different at home with the children gone, work and the demands of a job go on. You still have to catch the 8:05, and it can be a relief to have a little peace and quiet at the end of the day. It's different from the days when home was a two-block walk away. But for fathers, too, one way of life has ended and another begun. Now the needs of the generation past, like those of the new generation, must be fitted into a way of life that is no longer designed for them. Sometimes that can mean a heavier burden than the generations of the old family would ever have envisaged.

One woman in her early fifties said wearily, "You no sooner finish raising your children and get them started on their own than you have to begin caring for your parents. My father is dead, and my mother is alone. I know she's lonely and not well. My brother and sisters live in other parts of the country and can visit only once or twice a year. I live close by but I have to work. Sending the children to college is expensive. And what happens if I take her to live with me? Her whole way of life is different. She's used to doing as she pleases. Yet my husband and I can't change our pattern of living to accord with hers. She wouldn't be happy and neither would we.

"Maybe it's selfish, but we want a little freedom now to take trips, do new things, enjoy life while we still can. In a few years we'll be getting old too and we won't be able to enjoy our freedom. Yet how do I leave my mother alone? I try to see that she's taken care of, has what she needs, but I know it isn't enough. I know she's unhappy. And then I think, what will happen to us as we grow old? Our children will probably be living away from here. And they'll have their own children to care for. In any case, I wouldn't want to be dependent on my children. We have to plan to care for ourselves."

When needs no longer fit, obligations become burdens. The fabric of personal love is stretched because now it must extend across gaps in experience, do without the small familiarities which build intimacy, bind together ways of life that may touch each other only peripherally. In the past that woman would not have been working, her brothers and sisters would have been living close by to share the responsibilities, the children too might well have been living at home or raising their own families nearby. Most important of all, her life, her ideas, her ways of thinking would not have been so different from her mother's. People would have fitted together more easily. Instead of a break in needs, there would have been a shifting of needs, a taken-for-granted change in the emphasis of a continuing relationship.

Of course, people are living longer, and responsibilities that once encompassed five years may now stretch to twenty. And that may be a burden that costs a generation so high a price it can only be fought. It is not the extension of life but the extension of helplessness, loneliness, and isolation that weighs so heavily upon the fabric of family ties. Dependence on one's children has changed from a right to a special kind of charity. No one with pride wants to be an obligation or a burden, least of all on those he loves. When needs are too one-sided, one may not ask for anything without hurting one's dignity and self-respect. And so grandparents turn to their own generation for the give-and-take, the needing and meeting of the need that ties together the building blocks of living. Parents, it would seem, plan to do the same thing when their children are gone. The future must be served.

For children too the situation is different. Their dependence no longer implies the obligation to care for their parents in the distant future. Their obligation will be to their children and to their society. There is no mutual obligation except when crisis or personal feelings create mutuality.

This passion for independence does have its positive aspects. It avoids the conflicts that were once commonplace when grandparents moved in with their children: the acting-out of old grudges, the inevitable frictions and necessary accommodations, the tyranny of the weak and the exploitation of weakness. That system of interdependence did not ensure happiness, but then neither does independence.

People miss family closeness, yet they don't notice that their fear of dependence contradicts their longing for it. The right to need one's family and the right to be needed by them provided an anchor to windward. Families were no more all-loving or all-giving in the past than they are now, but they expected membership to be for life, with highly limited rights either of resignation or expulsion. That's a kind of security hard to come by these days—a security not of things but of people.

Only interdependence and the balancing of human needs can return to each generation that sort of security and bring renewed dignity to each generation. But interdependence must rest upon the true and valued contributions of each generation to the other, upon awareness that life and growth are a process in time, not a string of detachable freight cars.

5

A FAMILY NEEDS A HEART

In the memory of millions now living, the family was among other things a going organization. Like any successful organization, it had a head. That personage might be autocratic or democratic or upon occasion a nice blend of both, but he (the pronoun is obviously generic) kept the disparate parts tied together and moving generally in one direction.

Lucky families also had a heart.

I first heard the expression when a man remarked quietly, "Of course, my grandmother was the heart of our family. As long as she lived we were all to some degree tied together, because we were all tied to her. As long as she lived, we lived as a family." Rather sadly he added, "Families need a heart—that one person who provides the home base for everyone, who knows where everyone is and how everyone is getting along. Now families don't have a heart and that is a great loss, even though most of them don't know it."

Other people spoke with similar spontaneity on the same theme. They didn't all use the same symbolic word, but they all described the same kind of person. All but one of the people they described had been grandparents, and in all cases but one the person talking was already at or past middle age. All without exception spoke with an intensity of feeling rare in this day when family problems seem more prevalent than family feelings.

They had in mind no sentimental abstraction. They meant a person—a tough, real person, who had been the core of family life, an emotional Gibraltar who was truly the family's head, whether officially proclaimed as such or not.

"Let me tell you about my grandmother," said one man, now a grandfather himself, speaking as if she had just stepped out of the room for a moment. "She was the one who kept all of us going. She was a little slip of a woman who looked as if she needed a strong arm to lean on, but I think she was the strongest person I've ever known. Grandfather was officially the head of the family, but we all knew she was the one who made the important family decisions, the one who took care of things.

"My parents were both fine people, but they should never have married each other. Somehow one was always frustrating what the other wanted and they were forever pulling in opposite directions. I suppose nowadays they would simply have gotten divorced, and that would have been that. Maybe it would have been better, and each of them would have been happier; I really don't know. Anyway, in those days people didn't get divorced, not in our circle of life. Sometimes it was pretty hard on us children. We'd be overlooked while Mother insisted she had a right to work and have some life of her own and Father insisted she didn't.

"I was the oldest and I felt responsible for the three younger ones. When things got a little too rough at home, I bundled them up, put the two-year-old in my small wagon, and headed for Grandmother's. She lived three blocks away, and by some magic she was always home when we arrived. She never asked any questions, and she acted as if our coming was the most natural thing in the world. She fed us, put the baby to bed for a nap, and matter-of-factly began to bake a cake with our invaluable help. I could feel the weight drop off my back. Nothing seemed very wrong after all. We would talk along about the small everyday matters, what was happening at school, what we wanted to eat for dinner; it was all so natural and normal that I knew nothing really bad could happen—not with Grandmother there. She'd take care of it, and there was no need for me to worry.

"Later she'd go over to see Mother and Father. She never said much of anything about what happened, and I never asked. That was just another of those things Grandmother took care of. All that was important to me was that for a while life would be a little easier at home, and my parents would avoid the quarrels that made me feel as though they'd slammed the door on us. I still stopped by to see Grandmother every day after school. I'd chew on cookies and get around to whatever was on my mind.

"I suppose everyone took their problems to her. At the time I was only concerned with my own. But all the aunts, uncles, and cousins came regularly. On Sundays we all came for dinner, and Grandmother cooked until the table was covered with food. She had great faith in the efficacy of food for solving human problems.

"I remember when I had my first date with a girl, I was pretty uncertain on my feet. I went to see Grandmother. 'What do I talk about with a girl? What do I do if she doesn't like me?'

"Always practical, Grandmother asked, 'How much money have you got?'

" 'Two dollars,' I told her. 'I'm taking Marlene to the movies.'

"Grandmother pulled out her pocketbook and added a dollar to my hoard. 'Buy her popcorn during the movie and afterwards take her for something to eat.' We talked about all the possible exigencies of the momentous occasion, but I knew food was my ace up the sleeve, the port in a storm.

"When I grew up and got married, I moved away. My work was exciting and we traveled a lot, but as long as Grandmother lived, I went back every few months to visit. When I got a promotion or had a success, I always called her first. As long as she lived, I knew what everyone in the family was doing. Aunts, uncles, cousins—she was in touch with all of them, and because of her we were in touch with each other.

"Then one day she put on her hat, left a note for Grandfather that his dinner was in the oven, and went to the hospital. She died a week later. She hadn't even told anyone she was sick. That was exactly in character for her. Even her death was quickly and efficiently managed.

"After that the family drifted apart. There wasn't anyone to write, 'Your cousin David has a new job,' 'Mary is expecting another baby,' 'John's younger boy has to have an operation.' I guess it didn't seem too important after she was gone—or maybe it was simply that there was no one to tie all the threads together.

"Now that I have my own grandchildren I'm trying as

I never did before to bring some of this back for them. They live three hundred miles away, not three blocks, but these days that trip has first priority in my life. I never got really close to my own children. I was always too busy when they were growing up, too excited about my career, about making money. Now I see my son-in-law doing the same thing. I tell him, 'Don't. Get ahead a little slower and take time to know your children.' I don't know whether he can, any more than I could at his age, but I know I'm sorry I didn't. How I try to make it up with my grandchildren! I don't suppose they'll remember me the way I remember my grandmother, but I'd like them to have some of these memories. The truth is, there is no one now to take Grandmother's place and hold us all together."

A woman in her forties said, "I wish my children could have known my grandfather. They have no one like him to remember. They don't even know their own grandparents well enough for them to be important memories. I was an only child, but we were a big Jewish family, and I grew up surrounded by aunts, uncles, and cousins. My cousins were like brothers and sisters. But our grandfather was the one who really tied us all together. He was very religious, but he was never solemn about it. He taught us the services, and what they meant. He had a way of explaining that made all of us children feel a part of something very old but very alive and important, and as a part of it we were important too.

"He told us wonderful stories about the history of the Jews, about life in Russia, what it had been like to come to America. We listened fascinated. It was strange, but we never quarreled much when he was with us. We all went to him with our troubles and our special joys, but I don't remember we were ever jealous of each other with him. I don't know how he did it, but he made each of us feel special. And he made the past live for all of us.

"Only in the last year or so have I truly realized what a bond of unity he was for us. I married out of my faith and my family was pretty upset. There was a lot of friction and criticism, and for years I didn't see much of them. Only now that we're older, with our own children growing up, we feel a need to be closer again. We seek each other out, and the frictions that were such a big thing don't matter much any more. What we talk about is our childhood together, and there at the center, as if he had been waiting all along, is our grandfather.

"It's strange. He died before I married, before all the trouble. For years I didn't think of him, except for an isolated fragment of memory when something reminded me. Now he lives again for us, and we share a common past, a common meaning, a common perception because of what he gave us. After all these years our tie to him is our tie to each other. I wish my children could have had that."

They are much alike, these grandparents, as they emerge from the shadows of memory. They all had the ancient strength of endurance. They did not so much seek answers as live them. For them survival belonged to the family. Death, their own included, was simply an episode in a natural succession. They were the people everyone turned to for strength, for clarity, for judgment. They knew each person in their families, but more, they knew how every person must fit with every other—the conflicts to be compromised, worn down, placated, the irrationalities to be walled off or drained away. They knew that the delicate threads of human relationships could be irreparably damaged, and their first objective was to steer around the open confrontations that might tear their fabrics. Almost everything else, as they well knew, would finally mend; and if the cracks still showed, that too was life. Not romantics, they did not believe in perfection.

These grandparents, so vividly, passionately remembered, were certainly people of character and ability. They combined within themselves those qualities of head and heart that mark the great human being, and they wrote their history in the lives of their children and grandchildren. Yet they have gone, and no one is taking their place. Only one among those described was still living.

"My family is different," remarked a smiling, energetic mother of three school-age children. "No matter where or how often any of us—my brothers and sisters and me—move, we never lose close contact with our parents or each other. That's because of my father. He knows all the family news, everyone's successes and problems, and he sees to it that we know about each other. He keeps the telephone company in business, and I expect the U.S. mails have to keep an extra postman on account of him. At least once a year we're all home together—husbands, wives, and children. Dad and Mother say that's why they keep that big old house, so we can all be under one roof."

"But isn't that hard on your mother?" someone in the group asked.

"Not really. We all help. She says she comes to life when we are all at home. And my father feels that this is the way life ought to be—the whole family together sharing and arguing and planning. It really is fun, and it's important to all of us. The children love it and they get to know their grandparents and their aunts and uncles and cousins. But I guess it's more important to my parents than to any of us. Without my father I don't know who would have the time and energy to keep us so closely in touch with each other. Only my brother lives in our old home town; the rest of us are scattered all over the country. It takes a lot of planning and work to keep a family together now, and I guess only my father has that strong a conviction."

She is right: her father has to be a very strong person, because he faces obstacles that earlier generations scarcely knew. His daughter is proud of him, deeply attached to him, glad of his strength and conviction. Yet the necessities imposed by distance, the unceasing pulls of career and ambition, the sheer diversity and transience of modern life have brought a measure of artificiality to the effort to maintain a family in a way that was once simply normal. The bonds are there, but people must struggle not to free themselves of them but to keep them alive. The grandchildren will have memories of visits, but the old power of familiarity can be only a small part of their living past.

What is lost is precisely that intimacy of knowledge, that passion of experience that gave to those tremendous grandparents of another age their power and wisdom. These grandparents knew everyone in the family, and knew them out of the shared experiences that strip away pretense. The great ones, those that were heart as well as head, saw beyond what was to what could be, and tempered judgment with compassion.

There were family losses in the past, of course, those that by accident or intention slipped through the mesh of family control. I remember the story of a young man who came from Europe, found a job on a farm, and sent for his younger brother. By mistake, the brother wrote that he would land in New York a day later than he did, and when the older brother arrived the younger one was gone; frightened and alone, he had joined a group of his countrymen and gone to Illinois. The two brothers never met, for the hazards of travel made distance a formidable barrier. Yet because the concept of kinship mattered to them, the separation of the families was not final.

As travel grew easier and mail more reliable, the brothers' descendants found each other. There was no compensation for unfamiliarity, but the fact of blood relationship brought continuing contact. Relatives visited, wrote, exchanged family news. As always, one person by tacit agreement took the responsibility for keeping up the contact, but the last person to do so is now a great-grandmother. With her going the bond, so tenuous yet so enduring, will come to an end after six generations because there no longer will be anyone to be head or heart of the family.

There were family losses in the past, but today there is a loss of family. And that is very different.

6

MANNERS AND
MISUNDERSTANDINGS

Once upon a time people didn't talk about everything that came into their heads. It was considered bad manners, not to mention bad judgment. It was also unnecessary, since there were more reliable clues than words to a person's state of mind. The generation of grandparents that I talked to—at least those in the over-fifty group— were brought up with a selective chariness about words and a good bit of skill in decoding signals that never found voice.

It's almost forgotten now, but there was a time when personal matters—from how much money Papa made to the fight Aunt Mary had with Grandmother—were confined to the family. Every child was taught to keep his mouth shut and not to blab to the neighbors. Plenty of people still in robust health can remember their struggles as children not to tell a special friend what Mama had been overheard telling Papa about the arguments Aunt Effie was having with her daughter. The trouble with special friends was that they had a way of telling other special friends; and with frightening rapidity the story, considerably embellished, traveled home and boomeranged on its unfortunate chronicler. To be sure, adults suffered the same struggles to keep a good story secret— and sometimes lost. The whole process lent an air of intrigue and importance to even trivial affairs.

Nevertheless, personal matters were safeguarded with as much rigor as was compatible with the weakness of human nature, and serious situations that threatened scandal were smothered with more success than is popularly presumed. Other people might have their suspicions, but they were left with more speculations than proof.

Training in personal reticence was necessary in a small community where familiarity was lifelong. The problem was not how to communicate, but how to prevent *everything* from being communicated. People then did not assume that communication in itself was the answer to the perils of the human condition, and they had the peculiar idea that a few strategic misunderstandings were more beneficial than otherwise. I remember one woman who used to say, "If there's one thing I couldn't stand, it would be someone who understood me completely." To the modern ear, that remark has the ring of heresy.

Of course, no one talked about communication as such. Since it had not yet been elevated to the rarefied heights of an academic problem, people concentrated with simple-minded directness on what was being communicated, at the same time quite aware that this involved more than words. They recognized a whole range cf nonverbal signals, although they had never heard the expression "body language" and would probably have guessed that it referred to something vaguely indecent. They knew Grandmother was angry when she began to swing her foot, that Uncle John was impatient when his throat required frequent clearing, that Mother had had it when she started to knit twice as fast as usual. They knew that when the lines at the ends of Father's eyes turned up, he was feeling good. They knew when it was safe to introduce a special suggestion and when it was expedient to defer any boat-rocking.

They knew all these things from experience, because people were familiar to each other in a range of circumstances and roles. They knew each other over a long period of time and in a variety of aspects. While certain signals, like slumped shoulders or clenched fists, seem universal, true personal communication requires finer tuning, and without familiarity finer tuning becomes a lot more difficult. People can be quite different at work and at home, and they can use different sets of signals in each situation. When there was time and opportunity for observation of both, warning signs could be picked up quickly, with the additional advantage that, since nothing had been said, no one was obliged to recognize or respond to something better left unspoken.

The modern passion for verbal self-revelation has an alien ring to a quieter generation, to whom it gives much the same feeling as taking one's clothes off in public (which has its exponents now too). In a day of more enduring relationships it could stir up a lot more trouble than it resolved, as people were well aware. They assumed without apology that certain things in human relationships were important to know but wise to keep in silence. And disappointing as it may be to many of the younger generation, a lot of those things were not sexual. There were touchy spots in everybody's ego that didn't have to be exacerbated, and regrets and griefs that would not be assuaged by exposure.

In general, people didn't talk much about feelings, especially within the family. People had feelings; that was abundantly evident from their behavior. But talking about them was vaguely indecent, like talking about sex or how much money Grandfather had accumulated. Feelings were expressed in signals, and then as now in behavior. If Father got mad, he could use words with considerable fluency to describe what he thought of the target of his wrath, but he would consider it shocking and impertinent for anyone to discuss his "feelings of hostility." After a suitable cooling-off period he might acknowledge to himself that his outburst of temper was somewhat less than justified, but he would be chary of admitting it to anyone else. Any general discussion of the matter would be an unwarranted invasion of privacy. Children, of course, were rarely granted such privacy, but even they were accorded some degree of immunity.

The attitude is charmingly portrayed in a delightful song from *Fiddler on the Roof*. "Do you love me?" Tevye asks. "Don't I cook your meals and wash your clothes?" his wife retorts. "But do you *love* me?" comes the plaintive repetition. Emotions were expressed in behavior, in the small actions that carried their own message, not in words.

There was good reason for this. When people lived close together for a lifetime, there was less need for explanation and not much point to rationalization. There was a greater need for privacy than for self-expression. Physical proximity did not guarantee understanding or empathy, but it bred mutual knowledge; and because people knew each other better, they were far more aware than people are now of the delicacy and complexity of interrelationships. They lacked the touching modern faith in words, that purportedly can rupture and heal all in the same operation, so to speak. Nor did they make the modern assumption that personal change is easy and requires little more than a sympathetic push and a chance to communicate. In fact, they regarded personal change, at least for the better, as so difficult that it was more prudent to devote one's efforts toward living with things the way they were than toward any reckless demolition in the service of what they might become. For example, the efficacy of marriage as a medium for personal reform was not an unknown idea, but the experienced consigned it to the department of romantic literature.

To the modern young, all this can sound both cold and rigid, if not acutally hypocritical. To deny self-expression for the sake of peace in the family, or even out of love and consideration for another, is practically a negation of the modern credo. But the young have grown up in a different world, with different circumstances and problems. They must rely on words—they have small opportunity for the familiarity indispensable to understanding that tacit language, particularly with anyone outside their own peer group. In any case, their signals would be as incomprehensible as a foreign language to any generation or group or person lacking continued experience with them. Their problem is less a preservation of privacy than the necessity of making quick contacts with a widening range of people. They have no time for the slow and natural growth of mutual knowledge, and there is neither sharing of a past nor assurance of future continuity. Squeezed into those limitations, communication, if it is to exist at all, must rely on words.

People must have ready access to thoughts and feelings, and the facility to express them. Rupture of a personal relationship is less of a danger than lack of time to create one. Nor are the young so likely to experience the consequence of hidden ruptures that resurface over time. Inevitably they are less aware of the complexity of interrelationships because they have never experienced them through that enduring web of family ties, that intricate meshing of needs and demands that involved other generations and several families.

For grandparents and even for parents the signals have changed so radically that misunderstandings proliferate. The young talk about honesty, and generally interpret that as eliminating the screening process between the idea and the words. Older people call this rudeness and lack of respect. Even when they understand it, they endure it more than they enjoy it. As one grandmother remarked ruefully, "You never know what they're going to say next."

One father observed with a smile, "I don't see that what my children do is so different from what I did as a kid. They seem to have a lot of the same impulses and ideas that I did. What's different is that they insist on telling me all about it, whether I want to know or not. And frankly, there are times when I don't want to know. I wouldn't have dreamt of telling my parents anything of the kind. What they didn't know they didn't have to take a stand on, and that was better for their sleep and mine. The trouble with kids now is that they have no decent reticence."

An older woman visiting a friend said to her friend's son as she was leaving, "Don't get up." He didn't. The woman was hurt, and the young man was indignant at yet another example of adult hypocrisy. The older woman, uneasy with the ways of modern youth, was signaling that the small act of courtesy was important to her. The young man assumed she wouldn't have said, "Don't get up," if she didn't mean it, and assured his mother that otherwise he would have stood.

Manners are meant to convey respect, to smooth the abrasions of everyday encounters. But now telling a bore, "I don't want to talk to you any more," can be interpreted as honesty rather than callous rudeness. People of an older day did not suffer bores needlessly; but they had more graceful ways of extricating themselves. They called those ways tact and would have considered the label of hypocrisy ridiculous.

To an older generation, manners were and are the outward symbols of the rules of the game. Then as now there were people who complied with them out of expediency and habit, and there were others who saw them as the outward manifestation of inner sensitivity and consideration. Now the rules themselves have changed.

Most grandparents—at least those in their sixties— grew up in a time when it was taken for granted that older people taught and younger people learned. The theory was that the two processes were quite separate, and age was the dividing line. It was very nearly as obvious then as now that this was scarcely the whole story and that age could not be simply equated with wisdom, but this knowledge in no way altered the requirement that youth respect its elders and keep its observations to itself. Survival in and of itself was sufficient reason for respect, and if the individual hadn't garnered much wisdom along the way, young people were expected to confine such perceptions to each other. They might not act on their elders' advice, but they didn't challenge their right to give it.

Much of this sounds like hypocrisy to the modern

young. As one young man put it, "We respect a person for what he is, not for how old he is." They have neither the time nor the opportunity for what seems to them a game with obsolete rules. What they regard as honesty and candor comes through to older people as rudeness and indifference.

Grandparents, having reached an age where they believe themselves entitled to automatic respect—or at least to its appurtenances—now find they're supposed to earn it individually. That can be a lot rougher than young people realize. It takes a great deal of inner security to meet that bruising candor, that casual equality of manner, without hurt or anger. Some of the grandparents withdraw from the whole conflict, others try to meet the new ways with a kind of blanket assumption that if it's modern, it must be right. And some benefit, seeing that freedom opens ways for generations to learn from each other. They see that it's simply no longer tenable, if it ever was, for any one generation to assume it has all the answers, or all the problems either. No matter how differently each may look at them, all are involved in them.

The greater freedom of manners breaks down old barriers even as it creates new ones. The old formalities that regulated relationships between the generations did inhibit free and spontaneous exchange of ideas and perspectives; they emphasized the authority of the older generation and made it clear that the young did the adapting. More than one grandparent I talked to compared his present ease with his grandchildren to childhood memories in which a grandparent had been a figure of awe. One Southern grandmother, reminiscing about her childhood, observed, "I could never have played with my grandmother as my grandchildren do with me. I play games with them, sit on the floor with them. They come rushing up and jump in my lap, yell and hug me. I like it, and I think it's much better than the way I was brought up. I had to wait for my grandmother to pick me up. I wasn't supposed to play with her. I didn't yell or argue with her, and I was taught to say, 'Yes, ma'am, no ma'am' to her. Both the children and I are happier this way. We can relax together."

More than one grandparent fortunate enough to live near grandchildren spoke with delight of the stimulation and excitement of new perspectives gained from free discussion with young people. They found them intelligent, perceptive, exciting. They treasured the kind of relationship made possible by the new freedom. The tragedy is that so many grandparents do not have the opportunity to know their grandchildren in this way, or lack the resilience and the interest to take advantage of it.

Confusion is practically axiomatic when signals carry conflicting messages. Instead of communication there is a battleground, with signposts whirling like weather-vanes. It takes time to evolve new signals and new rules, and once evolved they become a part of the Establishment that will horrify a future generation some day. In the meantime individuals from every generation find their way through confusion and conflict with the built-in compass of those values that provide the true substance of communication, the manners of the heart.

It was a girl of twenty who understood what "the manners of the heart" mean. She had worked as a telephone operator for a summer in a vacation hotel where many old people stayed. One morning a lady in her eighties approached her.

"Can you help me call my family?" she inquired. "I keep trying and trying to reach them but I can't get them."

"Where is your family?" the girl asked.

"That's the trouble. I don't know where they are. They're traveling, you see—my mother, my father, and my brother and sister. I need to talk to them. I don't know why they don't call me."

"It's hard to call when you're traveling. You can't always get to a phone," the girl said gently.

"I know. I realize that. But I need to reach them and I don't know where to call."

"I'll tell you what I'll do. I'll keep calling different places through the day and see if anyone has seen them. And if they call, I'll let you know right away."

"Thank you." The old lady's face relaxed. "I feel much better."

Every day after that she came to inquire and every day the girl explained, "I'll just keep calling. Don't worry. I'm sure they're all right. It's just that it's hard to keep in touch when you're traveling." And the old lady would smile, relieved, and go away.

That kind of sensitivity is probably rare in any generation. But many of the young spoke with protectiveness of the old and helpless, and they had a gentleness and understanding that transcended obligation. It may not appear on television, but it's there.

I suppose no generation is very good at explaining itself to another. Every generation thinks it ought to be self-evident to every other. But never did generations need so badly to explain themselves to each other, to try to understand their differing experiences and perspectives. Yet they can scarcely make a beginning until they learn to decipher the signals.

Young people have to learn that reticence is not the same as indifference, that deference does not imply submission, that life experience may teach little or much but it does teach, and that even in an age of great change it has a changeless relevance. Older people have to learn that candor is not the same as rudeness, that casualness of manners is not synonymous with disrespect, that in a day of shifting, weakening structures of what was once proper behavior, the young must grope to find a new way. And both young and old must learn that each has something of great value to teach the other.

7

LIFE WITHOUT FATHER

Not too long ago Father was a figure to be regarded with respect, if not downright awe. The very word "father" evoked images of power that might or might not be tempered with a pinch or kindness or understanding. Such a redoubtable figure seems almost as obsolete as the kerosene lamp these days, and there is a general feeling that it's a small loss.

The old-fashioned father was, after all, a pretty grim fellow, long on commands and short on humor. He was generally assumed to be right about almost everything that concerned the family, and if there was an occasional crack in his omniscience it was better ignored. In the language of Women's Lib, he was without question a "male chauvinist pig." Tyrant and protector, provider and judge, he was a symbol of that grand old institution the family, and the power that shored up authority throughout society.

The individual father in the individual family might or might not have resembled Father the symbol. There is plenty of evidence that henpecked husbands and child-exploited fathers have been around for a long time, and considerable doubt that children, let alone wives, have universally subscribed to the Father-is-always-right notion. Nevertheless Father, as a symbol of power and authority, remained on his Olympian heights. The symbol itself offered a sturdy support for the most wavering man, bolstering his self-respect and, more important, showing clearly what was expected of him and what he could expect from the other members of the family. No matter how sadly an individual father failed to live up to that image of strength, there was a built-in framework that shaped all but the weakest and most callous. There was a structure of fatherhood which incorporated powers and obligations, rights and responsibilities, and which remained stable regardless of how well or how poorly the individual father fitted the pattern.

Then as now some fathers failed to support their families, but public condemnation of these fathers was swift and clear. Then as now some fathers could not establish their authority over the coming generation, but no one was in any doubt about whom to blame (it was always the children's fault). Then as now some fathers were more tyrants than protectors, but while people might sympathize with the unfortunate victims, few challenged the paternal right. The image of fatherhood wrapped the individual father in a protective cloak, providing a model for authority and responsibility that stretched far beyond the family.

That image has, of course, been weakening for a long time, as the old patriarchal structure of life became obsolete, another casualty of the urban life style, of mobility, of the demands of the modern economy. Father simply can't ride herd on the kids as he once did—because he isn't around. Even if he wanted to emulate the authority of his grandfather, he has only scant opportunity; and authority doesn't thrive on discontinuity.

The desperate mother who meets her weary husband at the door with a full account of the children's sins of the day is now frowned upon. Public attitudes now remind her that her husband is weary from a day of coping with his own problems, and warn her that her behavior may turn Father into a kind of executioner. There is even the implication that it may threaten her marriage. But many a woman today longs for the strength and sharing of responsibility that once were a part of the pattern of life. Not that she lacks the strength and capacity for responsibility, but she has to carry a greater share of it than her grandmother or her great-grandmother. Individually that might be a blessing or a curse, but structurally it is a new pattern for which no one today has been adequately prepared.

In the modern world the average father, if he is to support his family, must be absent during most of his child's waking hours. If he is ambitious, anxious to become a success in his field, he may also be away evenings and weekends, or doing extra work at home. His children will not be able to share in or understand his work. For them, it is simply an interest that he prefers to them, a rival for their needs and interests. The father will not see his work and his children as mutually exclusive, but to a degree they will become so, existing in differing segments of his life; and as his energy, time, and concentration are poured into the demands of his career, he will have only scraps of time, energy, and even emotion for his children. He won't see it that way, of course. Why should he? He will be praised and admired for his success, and his family will be proud of him. His children will either bury their resentment and follow his example or, as they grow older, will find ways to express their anger and avenge their sense of rejection and loss. It is perhaps not so surprising that many sons of the affluent have turned so violently upon the world of their fathers.

Even the most devoted father finds himself torn by the demands of a society that leaves him so little opportunity for relaxed, natural relationships with his children. His work is no longer of a kind that can be shared with children. When he tries to help them with *their* work, he finds all too often that he's out of touch with what their school or group is doing. In a way he is as alienated from their world as they are from his. Opportunities to do something together toward a common purpose become rare.

This division means more than just a loss of teaching and learning. It shrinks by that much the opportunity for father and child—whether son or daughter—to know each other. Close personal relationships are built on sharing, on mutual give-and-take. The five-year-old boy who can help his father build a birdhouse has given as well as learned, and his respect for himself—and his admiration for his father—rises like a thermometer in the sun. But in our culture we don't build birdhouses very regularly, and our praise of a child's efforts lacks the ring of authenticity when it represents an attempt to boost his confidence rather than a comment on his actual progress. Emotional growth, like physical growth, takes care of itself when the climate is right.

Opportunities for learning, for the development of self-respect and self-confidence, are in our society located to a great extent outside the family. The teacher in school is more likely than the parent at home to praise a child's first efforts in the acquiring of a skill. The scoutmaster is more likely than the father to teach how to build a fire in the woods or to construct a shelter from the rain. But teachers and scoutmasters work with groups, and they come and go. They do not often develop a lasting relationship with a child.

Our society demands complicated skills, not simple ones, intellectual rather than physical dexterity, specialization rather than integration of knowledge. The father's ancient role of instructor could not survive, and in its disappearance it took with it a great opportunity for paternal influence and the strengthening of father-child relationships. To some degree fathers have become strangers; and strangeness increases when the hours of commuting, the demands of work, the pressures of competition are thrown into the balance. Father is someone who leaves in the morning in a rush and comes home tired and preoccupied, but with luck may be able to spare some time and energy on a weekend when, like a visitor, he may share in some isolated activity. Even then his work has priority, and the children know it.

One young mother in a prosperous suburban community said wearily, "It's always a rush in the evening. My husband doesn't get home until almost seven, and by that time he's really tired and tense. I try to get the children fed and at least ready enough for bed so that I can sit down and have a cocktail with him in peace and quiet and give him a chance to relax. The trouble is that the children, like all children, are demanding. They want his attention, and he's had nothing but demands all day. Sometimes he's irritable, and then I try to shoo the children away and keep the peace. We eat dinner later when things are finally quiet."

Even for the more relaxed father who looks forward to

playing with his children when he gets home, the time is short and often uncertain. If his boss wants to send him on a business trip, he's not expected to refuse because he promised to take his children camping. It's not so much the time lost on any one occasion that matters, nor even a particular disappointment; it's the inflexibility of the priority. The children are also-rans, and they know it. They have no vital role in their father's life because there is simply no way they can participate in it. They receive the material benefits of his success and so they learn to demand things, taking things as substitutes for the sharing they couldn't have. And sometimes they learn to despise the substitutes. In their experience, affluence has brought things and robbed them of importance as people.

If children try to bridge their alienation by emulating their fathers in their own way, they may find that the ways of competition are structured for them. Competitive games that mirror adult values and make winning all-important sweep away spontaneity. It is more acceptable for a father to say, "I have to hurry home and watch my kid play Little League baseball," than to explain, "I have to hurry home because my son and I are developing prints from the pictures we've been taking." There is a very different quality of sharing in the two kinds of activity, and sometimes children are pushed to win not because they care for the game but because winning is the way to gain a father's pride and approval. In the true sense, that is not sharing at all.

Inevitably the father's traditional authority is eroded. No matter how he tries, he has small opportunity to set and enforce a structure of discipline. The harsh and hostile father can demand reports of a child's behavior and punish the child for his sins, or his wife can push him into that position even when he is neither harsh nor hostile. In either case his role is more that of executioner than disciplinarian. His children may fear him, but they can scarcely respect his authority, for the message he transmits is one of violence and weakness rather than strength and justice. He is filling only a fragment of the old-fashioned father's role. He punishes but he does not discipline as teacher and protector, and so earns fear and resentment from his children.

For the father who is neither harsh nor hostile, authority must rest upon respect. Unfortunately that requires consistency of experience, and absence is more conducive to fantasy than to experience. Fathers become more pals than fathers—by definition an abnegation of the authority role. The conflicts and rivalries between fathers and children are transferred to the world of work, where the most intense part of life nowadays is lived.

The interrelationships of men in business, where the stakes are power and wealth, are in many ways reminiscent of the interrelationship between patriarchal father and ambitious sons, with the power and survival of the company taking the place of the family's power and survival. In this world, men are described as tough, strong, and self-assured; their toughness is admired, their strength trusted, their integrity respected. In our society we admire and reward the man successful in his work; we rarely even think about his success as a father. If children don't appreciate a successful father, we are more likely to commiserate with the father, who certainly deserved better. The last thing we do is look at the values we have promoted and the priorities we have set.

Alexander Mitscherlich, in his book *Society without the Father*, observes, "The cultural behavior pattern of North America has meanwhile developed into mere contempt for the father. Present-day American culture is no longer motivated by rivalry with the father arising from ambivalence between respect and hatred of him. What is taking place is centered elsewhere, and incidentally includes a non-respect for the father which is associated with very little affect indeed."

Geoffrey Gorer implies the pattern was set with the settlement of the country and its waves of immigration. In *The American People* he writes, "The making of an American demanded that the father should be rejected both as a model and as a source of authority. Father never knows best. And once the mutation was established, it was maintained; no matter how many generations separate an American from his immigrant ancestors, he rejected his father as an authority and example, and expects his sons to reject him."

If Mitscherlich credits modern industrialization and an altered style of life more than the break with European paternalism, both these writers agree that the American father has lost his authority and his children have responded not with hatred but with contempt. However accurate these views may be—and they are obviously not universally true—they do have something important to say about the modern image of fatherhood. There are those who consider that image well lost, feeling that father's power is better used in promoting the gross national product than in pushing his family around. What they don't take into account are the ramifications of that loss. Father was not only the material provider but the symbol of authority and responsibility, a symbol that set a pattern for authority and responsibility in the society at large.

Mitscherlich talks about the "invisible father"—not the individual father who is literally invisible to his children much of the time, but the absent father-image "so closely associated with the roots of our civilization and of the paternal instructive function." That father-image has been all-pervasive in the structure of our culture, in our way of thinking, our values, our goals, our institutions. Our religion has been based upon it, our patriotism has glorified it (although Americans from the beginning found their symbol in a jaunty uncle rather than an all-powerful father). The father was the symbol of power—power that might abuse or protect, or both, but power that was consistent, pervasive, and above all legitimate. With the disappearance of that paternal principle, the legitimacy of authority itself is challenged; and in the inevitable crises that follows, we resort to violence to keep order.

For both the new and older generations the result is massive confusion. Many older people endorse our materialism but bitterly resent all the changes that have grown from it. They view youth as an alien race to be subdued by force or appeased when necessary, but in either case as a potential and unpredictable menace to the established order. It is not always clear whether they want youth to come up with magic solutions to the world's ills or to settle down quietly into the well-worn ruts of the past.

For the young the choice is little clearer. Some reject the past *in toto*, or at least think they do. Relying upon each other, they substitute brotherhood without fatherhood, and the group becomes not a transition to the responsibilities of adulthood but a separation from the past. For these young people the group becomes the parent, and it can be an oddly tyrannical one, invading privacy with a ruthless abandon that even the most authoritarian of fathers might find extreme. The revolt against the family and the past reaches out to a more encompassing conformity.

Brotherhood without fatherhood is a new phenomenon, one that may disintegrate even more drastically than the dreams of the past. Fatherhood was a unifying principle, a strength that made possible the difficult connections of brotherhood. I suppose one might with justification ask, why fatherhood? Why not motherhood? Perhaps the identification of strength and authority with the paternal symbol is, as some advocates of Women's Lib would say, no more than a remnant of the past. But that symbolism has deep and powerful roots and can neither be disregarded nor lightly changed. What is certain is that no transition has yet occurred, and the danger is not so much the change of an ancient symbol as the breakdown of a unifying principle. As the words themselves indicate, we still think in terms of family, and we have found no means of divorcing our new goals from our ancient roots.

Other young people seek to harness change to a purpose. Their very attempt to work "within the system" is a tacit acknowledgment of the importance of structure, of authority and responsibility, an acknowledgment of the paternal principle with emphasis upon its protective function. If structure becomes the tyrannical father that refuses to admit the necessity of change, these young people too will be compelled either to revolt or withdraw. Many of them believe in the idealism of brotherhood, but they seek it as an outgrowth of the past, not as a cataclysmic break with it.

What is not sufficiently recognized by old or young is that we are all struggling with the same confusion. The old expectations are losing their power to exact and enforce predictable attitudes and behavior, and new ones are not defined. With no clear premise of authority the whole network of responsibility and obligation is threatened, leading not only to disorder but to frustration and hostility. Life without father turns out to be more confusion than freedom, producing more apprehension than peace. At least that grim giant of the past provided someone to fight against, and that was apt to be more soul-engrossing than boxing shadows.

Since we are clearly not going back to the stern patriarch, our problem seems to center on the evolution of a new father-image. We want benign strength, protective power, and the wisdom to know when flexibility must permit new freedom and growth. And so we come full circle to one of the most ancient of human problems: the balance between freedom and authority. Yet we seem no nearer an answer than we ever were.

We might begin by trying to understand, in human terms, the nature of our dilemma. One of the ingredients of confusion is not knowing what we want, and it's not much help to devise Utopias when we can't even agree on what they should look like. It would help if we could set a few priorities about what we must have if the family is to fulfill its most basic obligation: educating the next generation.

We can be grateful for all the fathers who struggle not only to be providers in the material sense but to give of their strength and understanding to their families despite the rigors of outside economic demands. We can be grateful for all the mothers who somehow carry the balance of responsibility without substituting one form of family tyranny for another. We can appreciate the young who seek new paths and certainties in a world that clings indiscriminately to what was destructive as well as constructive in the past.

Most of all, we can acknowledge that fathers are important, not simply as bill-payers but as an integral force in the family. Children need fathers, and society needs the principle of fatherhood. The compassion, the sense of fairness, the steadiness of responsibility that were once summed up by that principle are qualities we sadly need. Perhaps our first step is once again to honor fatherhood by honoring those qualities from which we may some day fashion a new and more civilized image of paternal strength.

8

WHAT HAPPENED TO MOTHER?

If Father once symbolized power, authority, and responsibility, Mother was the symbol of love, nurture, and gentleness. Individual fathers and mothers might have had those qualities in greater or lesser degree, but the principle held firm: Father made life possible, and it was up to Mother to make it worth living.

Yet in our time the maternal symbol, like the father-image, has been obscured by confusion and contradiction. The ideal of motherhood has been ferociously attacked and as ferociously defended. A woman can be patronized if she does not have children and regarded as backward if she is only a wife and mother. If she tries to combine a career and motherhood her problems multiply. There are few standards for a mother to use as a measure; she is on her own. Fathers at least have the goal of success in work, with its rewards of money and prestige, but mothers have neither a clear definition of success nor any widely accepted means of achieving it.

Women have been particularly vulnerable to the sad split between the demands of the ego and the longings of the libido—between the need to be admired and the longing to be loved. Success and achievement in our society mean winning the competition in the world of work—becoming somebody, as we bluntly put it. We give less attention to success in parenthood, the process of helping children become first-rate human beings. That belongs to another segment of life, to be measured in any case by the children's material success. A successful wife is one so acknowledged by her successful husband, and a successful mother is known by her successful children. We admire the success, but we take the family contribution for granted. Sometimes in a burst of bias we blame parents for their children's failures, but we rarely accord them wholehearted praise for their children's successes.

Traditionally motherhood has symbolized the non-competitive virtues: love, sympathy, patience, gentleness, self-sacrifice—virtues both admired and despised in a dangerous and not very gentle world. Mothers have been left to reconcile these traditional virtues with the contradictory demands of our ever-changing society. As fathers disappeared for ever longer periods into the world of work and competition, mothers have been left more alone than they have probably ever been in all of history. Relatives are few, and made scarcer still by vicissitudes of modern mobility; and they are pretty much ruled out anyway as sources of influence and support. Neighbors come and go; those once-sturdy underpinnings, church and community, have lost authority. Mothers have books, the conflicting advice of experts, and, if they have the time and opportunity, they can always take a course.

One mother reminisced, "When I had my first baby, we were living in New York in a small apartment. My husband was just getting started with the company, and he had to work long hours. I didn't like to burden him with my problems when he did get home, because I knew he'd been working with problems all day; besides, there wasn't anything he could do about mine anyway! I had no family and no close friends in the city; they were all back in Illinois where we came from. There were times when I thought I'd lose my mind. I didn't know whether I was doing the right thing for the baby. Sometimes I didn't know whether he cried because he was sick or just because he wanted to cry. I'd begin to feel I was in jail, that I was trapped. Sometimes I'd leave the baby alone and walk around the block just to get away for a few minutes, and then I'd hurry back for fear something would happen."

This was an educated, intelligent woman who had been launched on a career of her own before the baby came. She had had dreams of success and of the rewards that came with it, and she had found self-expression and self-development in her work. But there was little stimulation in the monotonous round of her household chores. The rewards were entirely personal, and they were not always felt within her cocoon of loneliness and anxiety. The tedium she endured, the endless responsibility she assumed, were remarked by no one, probably not even by her husband, absorbed in the demands of his own work. Yet this is a commonplace situation, and with our customary indifference to common human dilemmas, we expect it to take care of itself.

Problems multiply as children grow older. With fathers absent more often than not, mothers continue to carry alone the responsibility of making the daily decisions, of meeting the children's daily demands. It is a responsibility hard to share with even the most devoted father, for the world of work and the world of home are widely separated, and the perspective of a father who spends a few hours a week with his children is very different from that of a mother who lives with them all day and knows all the small, intimate details that make up their lives. And it is not just a matter of familiarity. In his work a man is trained to define, analyze, and solve problems, to see decisions as part of a consistent, logical process with specific objectives. At home his wife has learned that problems are often too close and too personal to be easily defined, that solutions are rarely straightforward and practically never permanent, that logic is regularly violated, and that objectives should be approached with healthy skepticism. It is not easy to share responsibility when so much of the experience that is its substance cannot also be shared.

Furthermore, as the father's authority has been eroded, the mother has had to assume it. It is she who enforces decisions singly or jointly made, who permits or denies those myriad daily demands. Increasingly she sets the structure as well as the style of authority, yet she must reconcile it with those qualities of motherhood for which children have equal need: comfort, understanding, and patience. At best her role requires a high degree of maturity and self-confidence, but few mothers nowadays can count on the most favorable climate for sustaining these qualities.

Very early a mother encounters the influence of the school, which may or may not reinforce her own convictions, and the power of that third force, the peer group. There was a time when it was assumed that so long as one lived in the "right" neighborhood or suburb, where everyone shared essentially the same standards, the social environment would present little difficulty for children. Home, school, and companions would all be moving in the same general direction, and any contradictions would be no more than the usual human differences of age and personality. But now confusion has invaded even the most affluent suburb, contradiction and conflict have become commonplace, and the conscientious mother must struggle with two exceedingly complex and difficult problems. She must have confidence in her own convictions or risk being submerged in the conflicts rising about her, and she must have sufficient influence over her own children to inculcate in them the values she considers most important. When her husband shares her convictions and her influence, her problem is certainly eased and family influence is strengthened. Yet the mother is still the one who is directly on the spot.

Almost every mother can document the story. That weary question, "Am I doing the right thing?" is the tip of the iceberg. Beneath it are the corroding doubts, the impossible-to-answer uncertainties, the headache-producing confusions. Given any chance at all, children argue—as every mother knows—but now they can marshal supporting evidence from the world of school and peers. The script is predictable:

"Why can't I go to Jean's party Saturday night? Ellen and Kay are going, and their mothers don't see anything wrong with it."

"Because Jean's parents won't be there, and I don't want you at any party if the parents aren't there."

"What do you think is going to happen? You mean you don't trust me!"

The mother thinks of everything she has heard about drinking and drugs and sexual experimenting at teenage parties.

"It isn't that I don't trust you. But you don't know what can happen."

"You don't trust me. You think I'll get pregnant or try drugs."

The argument can be interminable, and there are only two possible endings: either the mother surrenders out of weariness or doubt, or she settles for a flat "no." If she is sure of herself, the "no" is likely to be accepted with covert relief under the surface storm. But if her response comes from the desperation born of being backed into a corner, she has sown the seeds of new trouble, regardless of the nature of her answer, for she has signaled weakness and uncertainty, and she knows they will be exploited. Children can forgive a parent for being wrong, but weakness sends them looking elsewhere for strength.

It is hard to escape the conclusion that much of what is called permissiveness these days is actually parental surrender. Permissiveness by definition implies authority, and while limits may be broadened and rules shifted, there are still certainties about what is and is not permitted. This does not appear to be the case in many families. Instead of certainty there is uncertainty; instead of a new conviction, a new direction, there is only the collapse of old convictions and the absence of direction. Further, the popularity of "doing your own thing" offers to both parent and child the absolution of personal responsibility. Only the requirement of financial support remains, and things become the medium of exchange between parent and child. In an affluent society that is no great hardship, and the child well provided for economically can even be said to come from a good home. But with nothing to rebel against, with no opportunity to grow their own inner convictions within a family, children flee to the power of the peer group. The peer group has not so much won in a struggle with the family as it has moved into a vacuum; and there is considerable indication that it has proven something less than a happy solution for many young people.

The ceaseless demands on a mother's time and energy, her emotional and physical investment in her children's growth, are for a limited time. Eventually the children grow up and leave home, and the beleaguered mother is abruptly an unoccupied woman. Her children may seek her help now and then, but on their own initiative and with no implication of continuity. Our society is quite clear on that point: no mother is allowed to "do her own thing" if it involves interfering in her grown children's lives and attempting to extend her dominance over them. Her husband has his work and may be more, rather than less, engrossed by its demands; he continues to be intensely involved in a world in which his wife can have at most a peripheral and subsidiary role. In the context of our time, she is still a young woman, vigorous, capable, intelligent, well informed, usually well educated. Yet the culture which has made so many demands on her now wipes its hands and says, "Your job is done."

Many women, looking ahead to that predictable moment, begin early to involve themselves in outside interests and activities, which means adding to their already exhausting daily round while their children are still young, but which also insures against the terrible break in continuity which says they are no longer needed. Even more, it offers escape from the essential loneliness of family isolation, from the monotony of unremitting demands, from the enervating doubt that the family is the medium for a woman's real self-expression. For no small part of the modern woman's dilemma is that her role as wife and mother is both praised and despised. Even when she is most needed by her family, she is haunted by the feeling that she is failing herself and wasting her skills, especially if her previous training or experience demanded imagination, creativity, administrative competence, or organizational talent. Certainly she cannot expect the recognition and praise that would accompany success in the world beyond the family. The old rewards—the love, concern, and honor of her children—seem dim and uncertain in an era that has little time for such matters. This can lead to a devastating form of self-doubt, which strikes at exactly those qualities which motherhood has symbolized but which are not traits highly valued in competitive struggle or aggressive action, and are not even regarded as worth the investment of an intelligent woman's time. Paradoxically, our society glorifies individualism as the supreme value, but has no time for the human values which distinguish the true individual from his machine-stamped facsimile.

That same kind of corrosive doubt affects many of the activities and concerns to which women turn. Community organizations and services to people are considered proper activities for women who are economically comfortable and have time on their hands. These activities are usually concerned with the care of people in one form or another, which often means they have about them an aura of "this is a nice thing to do but doesn't exactly have top priority in importance." The woman seeking to make a serious contribution to the problems of her community must also struggle with the feeling that she is an amateur. If she is not working for a paycheck, it is assumed that she is a pleasant and well-meaning dabbler who will probably do some good and not much harm. But again, her sense of her own importance is subtly attacked. Many women fight back successfully and win the respect and admiration of their communities, but they must fight not only for the issues at hand but for their own self-confidence. The values of our society do not spontaneously support them.

There are no ready-made outlets for the energies of the woman who does not involve herself in outside activities, no compelling needs for anything she has to give. Her time is a blank upon which there is nothing much to write. More than one woman seeks for ways to escape that emptiness in alcohol or promiscuity or transient excitement. Her relentless enemy is loneliness.

Thousands of women, of course, go to work. Many must work while their children are still young, and economic need resolves any inner conflicts. If a woman prefers to work even without the pressure of need, the fact that vast numbers of other women are also working ensures her acceptance by the culture. It is easy to understand why women work when their earnings are needed by the family, or when they have special talents, training, or special skills that may be in demand. Yet increasingly women work when none of these circumstances exist. They want to be independent, to escape the monotony of housework and child care.

The complications of handling a job and a family are sufficient to challenge any executive. The sheer organization involved in planning for the care of a family and fitting it all into the hours surrounding a daily job is no small feat. It requires the ability to shift almost instantly from one world to another, from the personal to the impersonal and back, to make endless small decisions and numerous big ones, to meet emergencies with a fine-tuned flexibility. A woman must be powerfully motivated to seek out this much responsibility and maintain it at such a cost in time and energy.

Between the needs of children and the demands of a

job there will be inevitable conflict, and one or the other must take priority. In most jobs demands are limited by time but inflexible. With children the demands may be flexible, or relatively so, but children have small regard for the conflict. For the conscientious mother, therefore, anxiety and guilt are often added to the daily routine. Only a fortunate few can afford the kind of child care that leaves them free of worry about their children in their absence; for most there must be nagging doubts, particularly in this day of drugs, delinquency, and sudden danger.

As one mother remarked, "No matter how carefully you plan, you can't be in control of the situation when you're not there. I feel pretty sure my children can handle themselves, and I talk to them a great deal about the problems and situations they meet at school and in the neighborhood. I go home directly from work, and my husband and I rarely go out in the evening without the children. Even so, I can never be sure that something won't happen—that my daughter won't decide impulsively to go off with a group of kids experimenting with drugs or sex. She wouldn't mean to do anything I had warned her against, but she's on her own until her father and I get home from work. That's a lot of responsibility for a fourteen-year-old. I suppose she could just as well get into trouble if I was sitting at home waiting for her, but that isn't much comfort."

The problem of priority lurks forever in the wings. Seeing to the needs of job and children and husband requires a balancing act that involves far more than time and energy. Emotional investment cannot be easily boxed and pulled out on demand like crackers off a grocery shelf; yet it is emotional investment that is needed, and like time and energy it must be split and somehow balanced. The anxieties of the job must not intrude upon anxieties at home; office rivalries and hostilities must not be carried into the rivalries and hostilities of the family. Success in a career may become a threat at home. The conscientious mother has an endless struggle for a balance rarely achieved; for the indifferent mother the priority is clear, and once again the children know they are the also-rans.

Whether women work or stay at home, they are entangled in the conflicts and divisions of a society that does not really know what it wants of them. The clear-cut role of wife and mother no longer fits our economy or our way of life. We reward it more with empty sentiment on Mother's Day than with continuing respect or evidence of solid need. Our culture makes tremendous demands on women when their children are young and their husbands are struggling up the career pole, and it throws them back on their own resources when the children are grown and the husbands have made it. It requires everything and nothing, and leaves it up to the individual to cement the halves together.

Yet a remarkable number of women have succeeded in doing just that. Whether they have divided their lives into more or less self-contained segments or have created a viable balance between home and work, they have managed to keep their equilibrium, maintain their homes and marriages, and bring up their children with reasonable success. The effort can exact a price; but the casualties may be a consequence of our confusion in values, our uncertainty of purpose, and our undermining of structure. Our society doesn't know what it wants of women, and therefore it can set neither clear objectives nor consistent guidelines. This confusion, as we have seen, drains a woman's self-confidence, her essential conviction of her own importance. If she meets prejudice in the world of work—and she does—that seems to say that her place is at home with her children. If she stays home, she is reminded that she is wasting her education, failing to develop her individuality, and spending her time on a job that could as well be turned over to a good nursery school or a competent housekeeper.

Some women solve the dilemma by resorting to one extreme or the other: they either stay home until their children are grown, or else they give unrelenting priority to their work and fit the children into whatever convenient interstices of time remain. The first alternative ignores most of women's present-day realities; the second ignores their obligation to the people they have brought into the world.

For most women neither is acceptable. Their problem lies in the balance between the two. How do they meet their families' needs, emotional as well as physical, and still retain time and energy for activities and work of their own? As one mother said with deep feeling, "No one who hasn't lived it can know the guilts, anxieties, and confusions that a conscientious mother with a career must struggle with. You don't want to short-change anyone, yet you're never quite sure you haven't. If your adolescent son or daughter has a problem, you wonder if part of the problem was that you weren't there when they needed you. At other times you think all the children were better off because you were busy outside the home."

Probably there is no perfect answer, at least in our present transitional stage. For every woman, the balance will be different. The question is which—home or work—takes priority at what stage. For many women conflict is inherent in whatever answer they give, conflict exacerbated by the contradictory attitudes of our society.

For a woman does not have a truly free choice. If she does not have children, there is still an undercurrent of social disapproval, though this is being diminished by new concern over the rate of population growth. If she has children and works, she is penalized by government policy as well as personal attitudes. If she has children and stays home, she faces not only the question of what to do with her life when her children are grown, but also doubt about herself as a modern and independent woman. Her rewards both at home and at work are circumscribed. If she has to fight prejudice in her career, she must also battle the social structure, social attitudes, and finally herself to affirm the importance and value of her ancient role as keeper of the home. The advocates of women's liberation, in their just fight to give women freedom in one area of life, may end up by denying them freedom to exercise their traditional role. Our culture makes that role precarious enough at best, and the wonder is that so many women still devote the best they have to its fulfillment.

With the loss of father as teacher, power, and protector, we have seen the premise of authority challenged and the strength of responsibility frayed. With the weakening of mother as teacher, refuge, and giver of tenderness, we are seeing personal concern, loyalty, and trust diminished and corrupted. Civilization would simply not have been possible without those qualities which we think of as constituting the maternal principle, and it is doubtful that civilization can be maintained without them. It is paradoxical that at a time when our society is desperate for the maternal qualities, women are wondering if they offer any true road to self-fulfillment, if they are not in fact inferior just because they are considered feminine. Much in our system reflects that doubt. The woman who teaches small children, giving them the concern, sensitivity, and patience that enable children to thrive, receives small recognition, in money or prestige, from our society. The woman who engages in research as a university professor is more likely to receive the accolades, the better pay. The lesson is clear: maternal qualities are lovely and lovable but not very important, and the woman who wants society's rewards had better look elsewhere.

Perhaps out of confusion, perhaps from long training in passivity, women have so far accepted this valuation. What they still do not realize is that, as upholders of the maternal values, they are potentially the single greatest power in society for a renewal of the human spirit, for change that can integrate the new without losing those qualities that protect society from an abyss of its own digging. In the past the successful mother kept her contribution within the family. Now she needs to expand it to affect society at large. If women would fight with conviction for the protection of all children, would demand care and concern for the old and helpless, would seek new means of promoting nonmaterialistic goals, they might bring new confidence and vitality to society and to themselves.

This does not mean that all women are or have to be concerned with care of people, nor does it mean that such concern is or ought to be confined to women. It *does* mean that instead of abnegating or downgrading the qualities which the maternal principle represents we should affirm their supreme importance, and women as a group should be in the vanguard of the fight.

9

CHILDREN ON THE LOOSE

There is a television station that solemnly inquires every night at ten, "Do you know where your children are?" Another station intones with equal solemnity at eleven, "Do you know where your parents are?" For children only one question remains: "Do you know where *you* are?"

Our culture prides itself upon being "child-centered." Our magnificent schools, our preoccupation with theories of learning and child development, our concern with the well-being of children, particularly children who have special problems, our recreational facilities—all would indicate that our pride is justified. Yet children as individuals are less important in our society now than they were a few generations ago, and they are steadily becoming more expendable.

Paradoxically, we admire and envy youth and yet

harbor a growing fear and hatred of young people and an increasing indifference to children. We have reluctantly made our peace with the illusory dream of perpetual youth; yet youth as an abstraction, as a state of being, remains for us a supreme value. But we are not very concerned about *young people* until their behavior creates problems; and then it is the problems that we are concerned about. Children as children are often forgotten; they are a part of the mass problem. As Mitscherlich observes, mass society is developing amnesia for everything which does not function like itself: childhood is forgotten and old age denied.

With all the great modern advances in health, nutrition, and education, children have benefited physically and intellectually; but with the trend of change in family structure they have lost what was once the most basic contribution of the individual family: emotional security and growth. The modern family may be fine for the economy, but it pushes children so far down the priority scale that they sometimes seem to be little but the prelude to a new generation, important less for themselves than for what they will become—and these days that outcome is by no means certain. Economically children are liabilities, and become increasingly so with the demand for greater skills and knowledge. The old *quid pro quo* of care between generations (parents take care of children and children care for parents in their old age) is weakening rapidly. The biological and emotional need for a child remains, but the strains of modern living attack the continuity of its fulfillment.

The satisfactions parents may experience in bringing up children are threatened, diluted, and sometimes destroyed by complex and confusing demands. When responsibility for a child becomes an endurance contest, child rearing is not likely to bring much satisfaction. It is rare nowadays to hear a parent remark, as one mother I talked to did, "Our son has been a joy to his father and me from the moment he was born. The happiness he has brought us is the greatest experience of our lives." When responsibility becomes too arduous and satisfactions too limited, the emotional need for children can be swamped by a longing to be free of the burden. Probably every parent has a fantasy of what his children will be like and of what the joys and trials of parenthood will be. But when disappointments outweigh fulfillment, the value of children and parenthood diminishes.

Hedonistic values have always denigrated the importance of children. The reality of their physical and emotional dependence, their vulnerability to early experience in the development of lasting attitudes, the inexorable process of growth itself have always required from parents maturity, continuing responsibility, and a consistent structure of authority and protection—none of them qualities that spring from impulse or accord with the modern definition of self-expression. They were based on old disciplines that were nurtured within the family and supplemented and supported by the culture. True, they did not guarantee justice, understanding, or sympathetic care for children, but they did provide limits within which a child could grow with some reasonable assurance of protection and continuity. As a very perceptive grandmother put it, "We were freer than children are now. We worked much harder, but we also felt that we were a useful and important part of the family. We had a lot more restrictions and our parents had much more authority, but we also knew what to expect, what we could and could not do, and what the consequences of behavior were. Beyond that we were free to explore, to wander in the woods, to create our own games, to dream and imagine. We had time and space. Now children have so little of either. There are so many demands on them. They're so organized and pressured, and at the same time they don't really know where they stand or what to expect."

Children must be fitted into a society that reserves the old disciplines—hard work, tenacity, continuity, and responsibility—for the pursuit of wealth and power. The importance of competition and success are taught early and stressed relentlessly. While children have some understanding of competition and winning, they attach quite different goals to their efforts. Above all, they want to be respected for who and what they are in the immediate present, to be loved as important people in the lives of people who are important to them. Young humans are of necessity self-centered; their needs are too great for them to be any other way. They grow into concern for others as their needs are satisfied and recede in intensity.

But this is precisely the area of need that is most ignored in our society. We don't have time for growth, for the quiet savouring of close relationships; we don't have time for intimacy. And without that, children become a combination of nuisance and promise, objects to be alternately exploited, ignored, and appeased rather than people to be respected and taught and enjoyed. There is a sad irony in the attitude of some Women's Liberationists who protest the masculine view of women as sexual objects, but themselves see children as objects to be moved around like so many inanimate pawns.

Diminishing parental responsibility increases child neglect. Even the affluent family may leave small children alone rather than engage in an exhausting search for a baby-sitter, and while the community may offer mild disapproval, it enforces no penalties. Children may be given money and left to occupy their time with what resources they can find. Parties of teenagers without adult supervision experiment with drugs, alcohol, and sex, often in their own homes while parents are gone for the evening or the weekend. The message to the children is always the same: nobody cares.

As family structure weakens, children can only rebel against the absence, rather than the presence, of parental authority. And that is a very different kind of rebellion: it has no focus, no clear objective, no predetermined perspective. Its focus may shift: now the university, now a particular group, now a governmental agency; and it seeks not so much fulfillment as the act of rebellion itself. It tends to respond to immediate pressures, trends, and circumstances. It is a form of rebellion that for some becomes a way of self-destruction, full of despair born of the emptiness of having nothing to fight for, or of self-hatred growing out of a past that taught neither personal importance nor a groundwork of self-respect.

Where the family weakens, the power of the peer group, as we have seen, replaces the structure of adult authority. Like the family, the group can become a tyranny, but unlike the family it has no responsibility for consequences, provides no continuing structure for security, assumes no institutionalized obligations. It is vulnerable to dominance by one strong individual, more responsive to immediacy than to continuity, to impulse than to plan. While the ascendancy of the peer group is not a new phenomenon, the current development of its power outside the authority of family and school is qualitatively different; for the group has become, not a channel of interim rebellion nor a bridge from childhood to maturity, but a way of life in itself, a negation of the past and a disruption of continuity with the future. Yet its values remain essentially those of childhood, stressing immediate gratification divorced from the processes of growth. When it seeks to become the source of individual identity, it in fact negates the reality of growth.

The influence of the one-generation group in a time of such massive and rapid change is inevitable. Group members share experiences that they feel are unique to this moment in time, and turn to each other for the understanding they feel they cannot share with people of another generation. Yet it is easy to exaggerate the extent of the differences, for human needs remain pretty much the same. It is how they are met—which ones are gratified as important and which denied, what drives are deemed legitimate and what forbidden—that create abysses between people as well as generations. We too often confuse outer appearance with inner reality. A young man may dress in odd fashion, wear his hair long, use a vocabulary that sounds like an alien language, and find pleasure in a kind of music that sounds like noise to his elders, yet still hold to standards of integrity, concern for others, and personal responsibility. He is not only comprehensible to people of any generation who share such standards, he is closer to them than to people who share his outward appearance but not the inner convictions.

Children come into the world with common needs that vary in intensity but not in nature. We acknowledge the common physical needs; but children also have emotional needs, especially for adults (whether parents or parent substitutes) who are models with whom they can identify. They need parents as people for personality growth as much as they need food for physical growth.

The process of identification is complex and time-consuming, and it requires continuity, parental protection, and parental concern. It is always personal. No small child can successfully identify with a group, a succession of adults, or an adult who is indifferent to him. He must for his own survival as a person be important to someone on whose protection he can rely and whose authority he can use as a guide. When a child successfully identifies with a parent or parents, he carries part of the past within him, and no amount of social change will alter that. He can destroy the past only at the cost of destroying himself.

Children's needs have not changed, but our concern in meeting them has. Fatherhood has become a sometime thing, motherhood a series of obstacles and endurance tests, and we have eliminated the supplementary aid of kin. But a child's need negates the quick and simple solution, the convenient if transient alternative, the mass approach. Children are personal and individual, and personality and individuality are grown from birth; the true individual continues to grow all his life.

A child's need for personal contact cuts across the pace of modern living because it cannot be rushed. When we push children to meet demands for which they are not ready, we destroy a part of personality. When we make the meeting of those demands the price for our approval, we sabotage the self-confidence upon which all later judgments and actions must be grounded, making it clear that we don't respect the child's pace of learning and growing because it interferes with the adult pace of doing and achieving. If speed is our goal, children must be content with scattered pieces of our time and attention.

Once the family was the forge where character was hammered out of human raw material. People knew how complex human relationships were because they experienced them. They knew ideal relationships did not exist, that life was made up of approximations, that relationships change over time, and that it is their direction that indicates their quality—toward greater cohesion and satisfaction of mutual need, or toward increasing disintegration and mutual frustration.

The endless intellectual discussions of human relationship, the groups—certain encounter groups, for instance—that strive for instant intimacy, in a vacuum divorced from past and future, are certainly reflections of the modern family's failure to provide those essential relationships and foster the growth of identification for its children. The idealized nature of the relationships sought by many young people is indicative of unmet needs. Young people seek from each other concern, loyalty, and sympathy with seemingly little awareness that these grow out of an experience which is marked also by hatred, jealousy, anger, and self-indulgence. Yet anyone who has experienced close family relationships would have such awareness. He would know that these relationships never achieve perfection, that they require the ability to give as well as the need to be given to, and that they also require order and structure.

There are still great numbers of parents who refuse to follow the priorities of our changing society at the expense of their children's needs. But for them, our society would be far more chaotic than it is. Yet we make that kind of choice exceedingly difficult for parents by making small allowance for the needs of children as individuals. When their needs conflict with the dominant pressures and demands of our culture, it is usually the children who lose. If things can be standardized and produced on a mass basis, why not children? Things can be quickly bought and offered as substitutes for concern and attention. A bewildered father says. "I don't understand why my children aren't happy. I've given them everything they wanted. They have all the things I never had when I was growing up, and still they're not satisfied." Affluence combined with a "do your own thing" philosophy can deprive children of parents as effectively as the plague, and for children far less comprehensibly.

It does something else: it diminishes the expectation that reaching a goal will require struggle and effort. In the past, economic struggle tended to promote family cohesiveness because its purpose was visible to family members and shared by them.

Children worked to help themselves and the family. But a modern father's career goal is hard for children to see, though money to buy things seems to appear without effort like manna from heaven. The work involved in earning money is invisible to children, and a father's job becomes an abstraction with no purpose meaningful to them.

The pattern tends to carry over into other areas of life, so that children grow up with the feeling that what they want should come easily to them. When that does not happen, it is understandable that they should feel cheated. They have been taught the primacy of their own desires, at least for the things money will buy. It is easy—but dangerous—to assume that this primacy should apply in every area of life.

People need to struggle for something if life is to have meaning and richness for them. Struggle is an essential ingredient in meaningful human relationships. Children struggle with parents, with brothers and sisters, and with other children to achieve what they want, and out of the process they learn and grow within themselves. Struggle remains a part of meaningful relationships all our lives, an essential part of emotional growth; we need the friction of opposition to make a goal worthy of achievement.

With children we do two contradictory things, both of them more fruitful for adult than for children's needs. We hand things to children, sometimes with overwhelming superfluity, until they have nothing left to want; or we demand from our children a competence, independence, and achievement that may be crushing, reflecting as it does not the child's needs or desires but those of the adult. The student who escapes into drugs or even commits suicide rather than admit failure may be paying the price of such a crushing demand. In both cases adult motives are suspect, and in both cases constructive struggle for something the child wants is denied.

The results are reflected in the demands of some young people for instant success. The monumental sin is frustration. Youth frustrated may turn to violence—and has. But violence is the small child's reaction to wish-negation before he learns the discipline of struggle and effort. Youth frustrated may give up the goal altogether and turn to something else—another reaction typical of the small child before growing integration of personality steadies and strengthens a chosen objective. A life without purpose worth struggling for is meaningless; and there are young people who, in the absence of such purpose, settle in despair for transient experience or the artificial stimulation of drugs.

Lethargy is another problem that affects growing numbers of young people. At a period of life when their energy would normally be at its peak, they drift. The satisfaction of even their material wants does not seem to be worth consistent effort. The very real problems of society are frequently blamed for this failure of purpose; but society began at home, and the hopeless young learned some if not most of their hopelessness early in life.

We value most what we have had to struggle for. But our culture has deprived many children of the opportunity, the necessity to struggle with any hope of achievement. Children have always been too wise to value things more than people. But too often we give them things and leave them to search hopelessly for the sense of self-value that grows out of being important to important people.

Even so basic a thing as sex should be struggled for—it gains value and meaning from the taboos with which cultures and religions have surrounded it. The sexual revolution may have loosened repressions, but it has also swept away a good deal of romance, glamour, and excitement. Sex just doesn't seem all that important. Freud remarked, "It can easily be shown that the psychic value of erotic need is reduced as soon as its satisfaction becomes easy. In times in which there were no difficulties standing in the way of sexual satisfaction, such as perhaps during the decline of the ancient civilizations, love became worthless and life empty, and strong reaction-formations were required to restore indispensable affective values."

Affluence has not been an unmixed blessing, nor do the children of affluence find life so much easier. Young people who voluntarily return to the ways of poverty and seek with others like themselves a family relationship seem to be acting out deprivation when it is sadly already too late. The turning away from material goals on the part of many young people is certainly a reaction to the emotional bankruptcy of a materialism that has become for many in our society the only goal.

The power of the peer group springs mainly from the willingness of industrial, urban society to sacrifice human values to material progress. The undermining of family structure and of personal responsibility has hit children with special force, not only because of their vulnerability but because personal values are the stuff of life to them. Yet young children are not very peer-group minded. They are far too conscious of their own weakness for that. They depend upon adults for strength and protection, and they feel safe only when adults demonstrate in everyday life that they are reliable and are using their strength for a child's protection. Children learn much from each other, but only when adult structure provides protection and adult feeling determines the emotional climate.

Much of this was taken for granted in the days when the needs of parents and children approximately meshed. They could never be a perfect fit, but with some adjustment and a little pulling and hauling on both sides they could synchronize pretty well. In our day parents have to do most of the adapting; they can't always compromise a child's basic needs without causing him lasting loss. Emotional needs, like physical needs, cannot be postponed without structural damage.

This is the tragedy of children in our society. They are so easily pushed aside, and the pushing can be glibly rationalized. The commands children hear are negative: don't interfere with your parents' interests, don't demand attention that will restrict your parents, don't be dependent beyond the limits your parents set. Those commands cannot be broken by children no matter how hard they try, because their fulfillment rests with adults, not children. The rage, frustration, and hopelessness engendered by this authority that appears to be nonauthority are perhaps the hardest of all for children to bear. It turns them into nonpeople.

Yet children ask for adult authority because it means protection and concern. Nonauthority does not give children freedom; it deprives them of the chance for freedom. The violence with which some of them react to the impersonal authority of school and society is connected to this deprivation. The attraction of drugs that offer immediate escape must be in their seeming a substitute, however illusory, for childhood need denied. The growing appeal of fundamentalist religion to many young people must have similar roots. It offers certainty, protective authority, faith in the never-relaxing concern of a loving Savior. This is not a permissive creed, and its tenets require standards of behavior that make no concession to the modern day.

Nonauthority comes close to destroying a child. It serves adult convenience, with the superficial appearance of giving. But in substance it is the reverse of giving, and children live on substance, not appearance. In a culture in transition, when traditional rules and structures break down, people require stronger inner controls than in times of social stability. When both inner and outer controls weaken, people are left to drift. Whether they seek escape in drugs, violence, destructiveness, passivity, or conformity to a new tyranny, they reflect a common need, a very ancient human need that no modern scientific advance has altered.

It cannot be accident that our society focuses upon youth and forgets children. We seem to assume that people come into the world full-grown. We attribute the restlessness, despair, and emptiness of many young people to everything but the losses of their own childhoods; we assume they have no past. The numbers of children increase, and we begin to see them as mass. They are problem or promise—more abstractions than people.

When we forget the importance of children, we attack our own humanity; when we depersonalize them, we depersonalize ourselves. What we are in a better position to see than any society in history is that, once the daily struggle for physical survival recedes, emotional survival is the only means of making life worth living. And emotional survival, like physical survival, begins with birth.

Children without parents might indeed create a society without hope. The fear that begins to seep through our confident culture may be at heart a fear of our own making.

10

ONCE THERE WAS A COMMUNITY

Once upon a time there was a living entity called a community. People didn't think much about it because they had been born into it, lived in it, and most of them would probably die in it. It was like breathing—worthy of notice only when it wasn't there. In cities it existed in neighborhoods where people lived most of their lives in the same houses or apartments, were of much the same ethnic background, and shared the same religion. But its archetypical example was the small town, which like the city neighborhood was generally homogeneous.

Plenty of the grandparents I talked to remembered what it had been like to live in an old-fashioned small town—and they smiled when they remembered. You always had to watch out for what people would think of you; if you were a young girl, you had to be careful of your reputation. Women all over town followed a certain order in their housework: on Mondays the clothes were flapping on the lines before noon, and woe to the woman who didn't have her house and herself presentable by two in the afternoon. People went calling, and they didn't announce their coming in advance. A reputation as a good housekeeper was important; and there was pity, tinged with a certain smugness, for the husband who had to come home to a disorderly house. The minister made the rounds of his church members, calling in the afternoon to inquire about the well-being of family and friends. It was a mark of pride to have a fresh cake or pie to offer him, all the more so because his calls were usually unannounced too.

"He wouldn't dare to do that now," one grandmother smiled. "Nobody would be home."

"And if they were, they would wonder what he wanted," added another. "My mother would have been horrified if the minister had found her with her dress not changed or her house not dusted. Every afternoon as soon as the dinner dishes were done, she washed and put on an afternoon dress and she was ready for company. I don't suppose it would have occurred to her that she might be entitled to more privacy than that."

"In a way people had more privacy then than we do," said one perceptive grandfather. "Everybody in town might know a good deal of your business, but they still had to guess a lot. And you couldn't imagine strangers inquiring into your affairs. Now everybody, from the credit companies to the government, demands all kinds of personal information, and they get it. People used to talk about each other, but they wouldn't open up to strangers. Their talking was personal, but this modern prying is impersonal. I don't know that I wouldn't prefer the old way. At least my father got a lot of amusement out of keeping the neighbors' curiosity unsatisfied."

"It was all so different anyway," a grandmother recalled. "In a little town everyone knew everyone else. You walked downtown and just about everyone you met spoke to you. They knew if your brother was sick, and they asked how he was. They knew all about you, but they could be concerned about you too. My mother still lives in a small town, and she's had the same next-door neighbors for forty years. She's alone since my father died, and these neighbors watch out for her. If they don't see her lights go off at the usual hour, one of them goes over to see if she's all right."

Another woman nodded. "When anyone was sick or there was a death in the family, people came with enough food to last a month. A neighbor or a friend would come in and cook the whole meal, or they'd take care of the children. I remember the great flu epidemic in 1918. Both my parents had it, and my grandmother was taking care of them, but the doctor wouldn't let her come downstairs or do any cooking. The neighbors sent in all our meals. I'd take the food halfway up the stairs, and Grandmother would come down and get it."

"People are a lot lonelier now," the grandfather said slowly. "We belonged to a town, and a good many people now don't belong anywhere. They can't have that feeling of being committed to each other that we did.

"I read about all the city youngsters who aren't in school, and I think what it was like to play hookey in our town when I was growing up. We didn't even have a truant officer, and we didn't need one. It was a big production to play hookey, and the chances of not getting caught weren't good. It wasn't just your parents you had to watch out for; if the neighbors saw you, they'd call your mother. You really had to get out of sight quick and stay out of sight. Besides, most of us went home at noon for dinner and that didn't leave enough time to make the game worth the candle.

"In a lot of ways I think young people are lonelier now too. We didn't have all the advantages and activities and organizations they have now, but we did have a chance to know people as whole people, under all kinds of circumstances. We knew grown-ups could behave one way at home, another way in church, and another way with friends. We knew a person could be patient about one thing and completely unreasonable about another. We grew up taking it for granted that people could be both contradictory and predictable. We observed them in all kinds of situations—reacting to each other and to us as children—not just in one facet of their lives. We knew a lot of things they didn't realize we knew.

"Youngsters now don't have the chance to know much of anyone but their own immediate family, except in bits and pieces—a teacher as a teacher, a policeman as a policeman, a friend of their parents as a friend of their parents. They don't have any natural way of knowing them as whole people. They judge a person by just one fragment, the one part of him they know, so it's easy for them to be confused or to assume he's a hypocrite when they meet up with contradictory behavior. At least we had a chance to know better. We knew there were as many different kinds of people over thirty as there were our age, and we knew any one person had more than one side to him.

"We were better off in another way too. We had a chance to try ourselves out with grown-ups who didn't owe us the attention we expected and had a right to expect from our own families. We could make relationships directly with older people. When you won the friendship of an adult on your own or worked with an adult without any help from your family, you could try yourself out as a person while you still had all the protections of home. You learned things about yourself and other people and you began to grow confidence in yourself.

"When I made a friend of an older man on my own, I got a lift I'll always remember. We had a common interest in astronomy, and we'd go to work with a small telescope he owned, identifying stars and constellations. That friendship meant a lot to me, and I felt proud and tall. It was something apart from my family, but it belonged to the security of the town.

"Children now meet a great many people apart from their families, but there isn't much independent and personal about it. Mostly they meet through groups that are organized and approved. Parents would be scared to death of an individual friendship like the one I knew, because they wouldn't know enough about the man to be sure it was safe. It just wouldn't be natural now.

"I think our young people are lonelier because they can't have that kind of human education. And because they don't have it, they don't have as much chance to know themselves. When we were young we knew the same people over a long period of time. They didn't seem to change much but they were always remarking on how *we* had changed. Now I see that this was a part of security: I could grow and change without losing a point of stability, a place where seemingly there was no change. No wonder young people nowadays feel adrift. Everything around them changes at the same time they are changing.

"I realize now how important it was to me that there was a whole group of people outside my family who could and did notice how I had grown and changed, people who could compare me with my own past. Almost always they followed the comparison with a question like, 'And what are you planning to do now?' It was so commonplace that none of us thought about it, but those people were tying together my past, my present, and my future, telling me that on the basis of my past they expected certain behavior from me in the present and future. That was a powerful force, a lot more powerful than most people understand.

"It could work against some families, of course. We had our three or four 'worthless families,' like all towns. Nobody expected much from their children because everyone assumed they'd be like their parents and their grandparents before that. As my own grandfather used to say, 'Those Baileys have never been any good. They're all lazy and shiftless.' When a solid family in our town adopted one of the Bailey children, the consensus was that no good would come of it because that girl was still a Bailey and she was just plain doomed to act like one, adoption or no. As I remember, she didn't turn out too badly, but she moved away when she grew up so I don't know what became of her.

"The town's expectations would be a kind of strait-jacket that wasn't always fair. Since the teachers pretty much shared them, there wasn't much way a child could escape them. On the other hand, the town protected those same children in lots of ways. They had to go to school; they had to be fed; they had to have clothes to keep warm. I guess the town wasn't very generous, and to ask for town welfare was certainly a disgrace. But we didn't have children going hungry or staying out of school either. Those kids belonged to the town, and the town in its own way took care of its own."

That grandfather described a whole way of life that lives now chiefly in the nostalgia of personal memories. Small-town America was most if not all the things that have been said of it: narrow in interests, dull, intolerant of difference, ingrown, and petty. It was also protective, loyal, personally involved, and personally committed. It could be surprisingly tolerant. I remember my surprise when I learned that a couple I had known all my life were not legally married. My mother explained, "Mr. Jones couldn't get a divorce from his wife so he couldn't marry Lucy. But they've lived together for twenty-five years and they're very nice, respectable people. Everyone understands that they're just the same as married."

The small town could be tolerant in ways that are no longer possible. I remember a respected citizen of my home town who had periodic rages set off by seeming triviality. Everyone, including his employer, knew that he was "peculiar"; as they explained, he had been that way all his life. When he blew up at someone for no reason people shrugged and said, "Don't pay any attention. That's Sam. He's always been that way. It doesn't mean anything." The result was that he kept his job, supported his family, took his part in the town's activities, and was respected for what he could do.

In today's impersonal society Sam would almost certainly lose one job after another. In our hectic surroundings, his behavior would be exacerbated; without the familiar support he would lack the indispensable respect that bolstered his self-esteem and gave direction to his life. He would in fact probably have spent some time in a mental hospital. But that town knew him as a person, not as an employee or a patient or a case. People moved around his "peculiarity" without attributing any great importance to it. They were not being noble or understanding; it was quite simply a part of life. Almost everyone had some kind of peculiarity; Sam's was just a little more so.

Such quiet acceptance has gone with the knowledge of people as whole persons. An employer has to think of his own business interests in a fiercely competitive society, and even if he were willing to accept behavior like Sam's, he knows his customers would not. The people in our little town would have been shocked and indignant if Sam had been fired, but customers now are strangers, and they would be shocked if he were allowed to continue. Nor is what happens to a Sam and his family any part of a modern employer's responsibility. He couldn't take it on even if he wanted to; it belongs to another part of the person's life with which the employer has no contact. Such impersonality can be more intolerant than the small town ever was, except toward its most extreme deviants.

Even unpopular points of view could be absorbed if the people who held them didn't insist upon promoting them too obviously. Some people didn't go to church, but they kept their doubts about organized religion to themselves or to any kindred friends. Some had unorthodox political beliefs, but they didn't shout their differences from the street corners. People knew about the differences and occasionally deplored them, but on the whole they regarded them as one more example of personal eccentricity. So long as the heretics paid their bills, kept their homes painted, raised their children properly, and didn't openly challenge the established order, their unorthodox ideas could be overlooked. It was not a stimulating environment, but it was not a totally repressive one either.

That live-and-let-live attitude did not, however, extend to strangers: *they* had to prove themselves, for with strangers there were no common memories to cushion the clash of opposing ideas and styles of life.

In many ways the town operated like a family, and that was no coincidence. The small town was made up of families, and most of its beliefs and actions were shaped by that fact. The great events of life were personal: births, marriages, deaths—they bound people together in a common experience, a mutual awareness of the rhythm of life. Like a family, a town had its conflicts, rivalries, jealousies. It could be cruel and kind, bigoted and tolerant. It had its social distinctions: men who had more or less power, groups that had more or less prestige, families who were more or less important—and those distinctions caused resentments, then as now. But people knew each other regardless of the distinctions—their rivalries existed within a framework of mutual belonging, and there were ties to balance divisions. People were involved with each other because there was little opportunity to be uninvolved. If they were less concerned about great issues in any official sense, they were more concerned in a personal sense with the people around them.

Although I saw many groups in various sections of the country while researching this book, I found only one community that still held to the structure and substance of this bygone way of life; and even there anxiety and uncertainty betrayed the erosion at its heart. It was a small farming community in the upper Midwest, its unity fostered by a common fundamentalist faith; and it still ordered its beliefs, its values, its style of living around the family-community symbiosis. Here the people were different.

The grandparents gathered with me on a Saturday,

giving me generously of their time, but they found it difficult to talk about themselves and their families. They took their style of life for granted. They did not talk about travel, or moving away, or new interests and activities. They didn't even discuss community affairs or problems, except to observe with a certain surprise that a group of Puerto Ricans had moved into their town and had lived quietly in one small section for two or three years before they were aware of them. In fact, what brought the group sharply into their focus was the request of the Puerto Ricans to join their church.

They welcomed them, but were also startled when the Puerto Rican group sealed their conversion with a gay and colorful fiesta on a sunny Sunday afternoon. This was scarcely an orthodox way to celebrate a solemn event, but as one of the women said with a smile, "That was their way of glorifying God. Who are we to say that one way of expressing that joy is better and more acceptable to God than another?"

They welcomed the Puerto Ricans into their way of life. Yet they did not talk of the Puerto Rican way of life. Perhaps they were more interested in it than they indicated, but it is also possible that it did not occur to them to draw comparisons with their own way of life. Their strength was drawn from their faith, which took for granted the standards by which they lived, and they had a strength that grows rare in a time of confusion and doubt.

Everyone met at church on Sunday and afterward grandparents, parents, and children were often together for dinner. The very young and the very old were a part of the family, and both belonged to a continuing process. Towards those outside the family there was not so much rejection as a kind of unawareness, because there was no place for them.

Religion and the pattern of rural living have so far shielded this community, but these grandparents worried about the future, about the divisive forces and changing values to which they could not hope to remain immune. They still had the strength of continuity, the security of belonging, the assurance of clear conviction, but they could not be sure for their grandchildren.

Their fears are realistic. It is hard to see how such continuity and certainty can survive in a world of confusion and change. It has already largely disappeared, but it has left an emptiness that we are only beginning to assess. As a structure for life it had many faults as well as virtues, but it gave to most of its members a place, a purpose, an identity that nothing has replaced. It made people visible. The fact that a man was known, was a part of the web of community life, gave him the importance of recognition. He might not care for his place in the life of the town, and he might improve it if he had what people used to call "get-up-and-go." But he wasn't compelled to struggle up the vertical ladder to achieve the dignity of a place, the security of recognition.

People still said, "Good morning, Joe. Is your boy feeling better?" People still stopped by his garden on a summer evening and remarked, "That's the most beautiful dahlia you've ever had, Joe." People still asked, "What do you think of that new assessment rate?" or "How are you planning to vote on that school bond issue?" One big expectation was that he own his own place—renting was for the new family just starting out, or maybe the single person. Owning the place where you lived was the badge of membership. Plenty of people never moved, and houses were identified not by street numbers and names but by their long-time owners. "Did you hear Joe has bought the Willard place? I hope he knows what it costs to heat it."

The town provided a man with visibility, and it gave him a structure for identity. Visibility was, of course, the indispensable weapon of social control, as well as the basis for security. There were all kinds of things people didn't do, not so much because the town disapproved of them as because the town was sure to discover them. Maybe people were more honest, more moral, more considerate, but they also had less opportunity to be anything else. Adultery required a lot more than a passing attraction. The sheer energy and planning required in a situation where men walked to work, came home for noon dinner, and were rarely out of sight of knowledgeable eyes were astronomical. It took a *grande passion* to make the game worth the candle.

Social control was a strait jacket and a protection, a teacher and a policeman, a guiding map and a prison. It was fair and unfair, blind and perceptive. It believed in absolutes but could make room for a little human perversity now and then. And always it was cynical about human nature: it took it for granted that, left to himself, the average member of *Homo sapiens* would indulge in all kinds of dubious behavior, and therefore it never willingly made the mistake of leaving him to himself. The eyes of relatives, neighbors, and anyone handy were its enforcers. Visibility gave a man importance, and it also made what he did and did not do important. Like it or not, he knew that he was no island.

Yet surveillance and control made him important even as they irked and restricted him. His sins were as important as his virtues, perhaps more so, because they were serious and significant to those around him. If scandal had a narrow stage, at least the audience was attentive.

That personal importance and belonging provided a

built-in structure for the development of identity. It taught the realities of what was popularly known as human nature. The relentless familiarity of people with people over time provided youth with a depth of experience that did not discourage dreams but anchored them to some of the facts of human existence. In that sense young people were better prepared for life than they are now. They had the practical, experienced knowledge that our modern life patterns provide less and less.

Parents had their worries and troubles with children then as now, but they had built-in protections, certainties, and outside supports that are now weakening and diminishing—in urban areas, almost to the point of invisibility. The family in the community of a couple of generations ago was not alone. It didn't have to seek help because help was built into its surroundings. As one grandmother said with serious regret, "I feel sorry for my grandchildren because they can never remember what it was like to grow up in a family in a small town as I did. They've lost so much."

11

WHAT HAPPENED TO ALL OF US?

Almost everyone over forty must have moments of feeling that he looked away for a few minutes and the whole landscape changed. For people over sixty things seem positively topsy-turvy. What happened to the world that seemed so stable and enduring? Where did everyone go?

There was the First World War; and after it came flappers and shockingly short skirts and bobbed hair and strange dances—and strange ideas. Then came the Great Depression, and families either drew together for mutual protection while the government fussed about who was responsible for supporting whom, or broke up as their men traveled the land looking for jobs. The Second War began and ended, and once again everyone looked forward to enduring peace, progress, and prosperity. A quarter of a century has passed since then, and somewhere along the way *everything* has changed.

An old lady in her eighties said wonderingly, "When I was a little girl, I lived on a farm a mile or so from the old Erie Canal. On summer nights when the windows were open, I'd hear the mule-skinners shouting at the mules pulling the boats along the canal. The other day on television I saw men walking on the moon." That was indeed a matter for wonder. The scattering of her family, the fact that her grandchildren were strangers, the contradiction of so much she had thought of as unquestioned truth—these meant confusion and fear and desolation. Only her great-grandchildren, still babies, were familiar; babies had not changed.

Like most people this woman had welcomed and enjoyed the progress—the things that made life easier, pleasanter, more exciting. She had traveled to places her mother could only read about, had seen radio and television bring the world into her living room. Like most people, she had not realized that these changes would in turn erase traditions and weaken the structures of life that people had relied on for stability—such as the family itself.

People have not changed, but the structures they relied upon have. The family of that woman, now in her mid-eighties, lived in a farming community. They raised most of their food. What they had to buy was purchased at a nearby village or from a traveling store, a horse-drawn van that arrived once a week unless the weather was bad. They ordered most of their clothes from a mail-order catalogue or made them. On occasion a dress-maker came in for the day. They had no fear of power shortages because they had no electricity; they didn't worry about the unreliability of plumbers because they had no plumbing. They made their own repairs or used the help of their neighbors. They were not totally self-sufficient, but there were few things that could paralyze their lives or threaten the rhythm of their existence.

In crises, birth and death and illness, they sent word to the local doctor, who drove to the house winter or summer, night or day. Most of them never saw a hospital, and many died who now would live; but people accepted that as they accepted the revolution of the seasons.

Their feelings of powerlessness concerned the caprices of nature and the inevitable catastrophes of life and death. In these they turned to religion, seeking in divine strength the power they did not have. They had no feeling of being at the mercy of impersonal social forces, since the social forces they were concerned with were scarcely impersonal. To these people "government" meant their town or county governing board—the government that most directly and obviously affected their lives and property, and that more likely than not was manned by their neighbors or people they'd gone to school with. They were aware of the Federal government, and the local newspapers carried rather more discussion of national issues than small-town newspapers do now, because there was no other source of information available to most people. These national issues were rarely of any direct, immediate concern to the citizens who might argue about them, and they would have laughed at the idea of being victims of a vast government bureaucracy. When they felt victimized, the wrong was personal and the aggressor known.

They knew that the rest of the world existed; but they didn't travel much, and fifty miles was a big trip. What they saw on their travels differed little from what they already knew about; and though a city might be impressive, it had little impact on the way they lived and thought.

A farmer worked long, hard hours, but he worked close to home, coming in for dinner at noon. His sons helped him in the fields, and his daughters helped their mother—who worked long, hard hours too—in the house. Everyone understood the work of everyone else, and the need for help was specific and obvious, as were its results. Roles were clear, and the whole family was engaged in a joint endeavor, as the food on the table gave evidence.

Everyone knew everyone else. They were all neighbors, fellow church members, homogeneous in background, in ways of living and thinking. Religion was an important unifying force, the expression and enforcer of what was and was not acceptable behavior. The church was the center of the community and its moral custodian.

Such a structure of life promoted certain values, and responsibility and reliability were high on the list. Cows had to be milked every day, other animals fed and cared for, crops sown and reaped, food grown and prepared; such unremitting demands permitted no holidays. But a man didn't lightly give up a good farm, and he expected it to stay in the family. He worked as much for his children and grandchildren as for himself.

Responsibility to his work was almost synonymous with responsibility to his family; he did not think of them as separate. The work ethic was supreme, family survival depended on it. Unreliability was not just reprehensible, it was dangerous; laziness was not simply a fault, it was a menace. Children were taught responsibility, reliability, and industriousness, but they could see the need for them; no one had to tell them where the food on the table came from. Obviously, then, their direct experience with money was only sporadic and peripheral.

Money could not have for them the same kind of significance as food grown by their own efforts. That food was grown by the family, consumed by the family, and belonged to the whole family. It was a shared, not an individual, achievement. Money as a separate entity, the reward of individual effort, was a minor part of a child's experience.

The structure of life in those days promoted self-reliance and interdependence. The multiplicity of jobs on a farm required people to work together for a common purpose. A wife and children were important economically as well as personally; the farmer without both was at a considerable disadvantage. The tasks on a working farm were endless, and the failure of any family member to carry his part threw a heavier burden on all the others. Here too reality was direct and visible, and a child grew up taking it as much for granted as the air he breathed. It could chafe and restrict him, but it also made clear his importance to the family: he knew he was needed.

At the same time he had to learn to be self-reliant. He was not a specialist, and he needed a variety of skills, but no one had time to supervise him once he had learned them. It was up to him to do his assigned jobs. If he ran into problems that were too hard to handle, he called for help; other problems he was expected to solve himself. Reliance on others was related to reliance on self; it was a matter of interdependence, not a simple equation of dependence-independence. And it did not have to be taught in words, for it was obvious, consistent, and tangible: it was lived.

The same thing was true of community relationships. You needed your neighbors and your relatives, and they needed you. You depended on them for emergencies, but even such routine as harvesting required joint effort, as men joined together and moved from farm to farm threshing the grain and storing it under cover. It was more important to get along with your neighbors than to like or dislike them; you would need them just as badly whether you liked them or not. Unchecked enmity could isolate a man, and that could be dangerous as well as lonely. People had their personal likes and dislikes then as now, but they had a different importance: the necessity came first, and the personal could be almost irrelevant.

Thrift and planning were integral ingredients in rural life. Every season had to be planned in advance with numerous possibilities allowed for: weather was fickle, prices could fall, a barn could burn. In those cases there would be little to fall back on except the help of relatives and neighbors and one's own savings, and relatives and neighbors would be much more sympathetic if a family had already done everything possible to safeguard themselves. Calamity that was no one's fault could happen to anyone, but spendthrifting did not come under that category.

Responsibility, reliability, persistence, industriousness, self-reliance and mutual obligation, planning ahead, thrift—these were the essential qualities for the old rural way of life. The respect of one's fellow men hinged on them; they were the dividing line of family worth. Since this was a time that placed importance upon "good family" and "good breeding," a child did not easily escape the onus of a "worthless family" or "shiftless people" whatever his own efforts. Other virtues were admired, of course. Generosity, love, loyalty, consideration of others, integrity—the whole range of qualities that lift human beings to special heights—were important, but not in the same way essential. They might make life worth living, but they were not necessary to survival; they were individual qualities, not social demands. Expectations were more concerned with behavior than feelings, however much the former might be assumed to include the latter.

This was a life structure whose goals were continuity, stability, and order. The family was the focus of life, and commitment to it was in one form or another life-long. Individuals had their rights, but in most cases these were secondary to the welfare of the family as a whole. Thus marriage was a family as well as an individual matter, the rearing of children was a parental responsibility but could include plenty of interference by relatives, the reputation of one member of a family reflected on all the others. Social controls were enforced by the community and the church as well as the family. Freedom, at least in the modern sense, was a highly relative matter. And, in fact, opportunities for revolt were limited, unless an individual chose to strike out on his own or to accept some pretty considerable risks. Channels for revolt were not built into the system.

To a surprising degree the same structure and values held in the cities. People lived in neighborhoods that tended to be homogeneous in religion, nationality, and ethnic background. Many newcomers from abroad brought with them a structure and pattern of family life forged out of centuries of family power and tradition. They too emphasized hard work, joint family struggle and achievement, responsibility, self-reliance; they too were a part of a web of community interdependence as strong as the structure of rural life. While money was far more important as a daily commodity in an urban setting, it tended to belong more to the family than the individual.

City dwellers might be more aware of the larger units of government, state and Federal, but they too were primarily concerned with local government. In immigrant neighborhoods the local politician was the focus of power—a very personal kind of power. In the cities there was inevitably more diversity, more strains upon family unity, more opportunity for individual revolt, yet the power of tradition and the strength of family structure held people together against the intrusions of the external and the alien. Religion was an intrinsic part of the pattern, enforcing values and standards, and impressing them upon the new generation. As in the country and the small towns, church and synagogue were social centers and moral custodians.

This was the kind of world great-grandparents—people now in their eighties—knew as children. But by the time they had married and were raising their own families, change had come. People were moving from the country into towns where new jobs were opening up, where work was not so hard and confining, where there was more protection from the uncertainties of the elements. Living was easier, what with electric light, central heating, indoor plumbing. People tended, however, to live in towns close to where they had grown up, and they brought with them the values, beliefs, and standards they had learned as children.

Like the farming community, the small town was full of familiar faces; people knew each other over a lifetime. Yet the town offered more diversity. There were friends who had not known each other as children. There were more and different churches. Even in towns with homogenous populations, representatives of other cultures or even races filtered in—a family or two from Southern Europe, a black family—not enough to shake the dominant white Protestant philosophy, but elements of diversity nonetheless. Men did different kinds of work, and while many of them came home for dinner at noon, their work was no longer visible to the children. Women remained at home unless they married, and even then it was not unusual for them to continue living with their parents.

Instead of the one-room country school, children went to larger schools where they were separated by age, with a different teacher every year instead of the same one for every grade. Their education was broader, even if it didn't include any markedly new ideas; they knew more children, and however narrow the range of difference among them, there was more difference. They could join in school activities, go to parties, form clubs, and find a social life apart from family and church.

Parents too joined organizations that were often allied with a church, but not an integral part of it. While family and church remained the center of their activities, they made friends apart from both. Men had business contacts that took them away from their families, and, in time, friendships in which their families did not share.

Yet the small town supported the old controls—in many ways more effectively than the rural community. A town afforded less privacy, and the neighbors let little escape their vigilance, night or day. A light burning at 2 A.M. was sure to alert some wakeful citizen. Nor did the town consider privacy an inalienable prerogative: there was a silent and continuing tug-of-war between the inquisitiveness of the populace and the determination of the family, let alone the individual, to keep personal business personal. The fact that just about everyone played both roles was no deterrent to the zest for the game.

The small town believed in responsibility and reliability, in hard work and thrift, in planning and self-reliance, in orderly processes and sober respect for the past. People were more interested in "getting ahead" because more opportunities to do so were appearing, easier to come by and more enticingly varied: you didn't have to be a millionaire to buy a bigger house, take a trip to Washington, or own that new marvel, an automobile. Nevertheless respectability was still essential to self-respect, and that meant working six days a week, paying your bills, keeping a clean house, going to church, taking care of your children and keeping your marriage vows.

Interdependence was still a way of life although its urgency had diminished. Parents took care of their parents, and when the older people could no longer manage for themselves, their children brought them into town to live with them. Relatives saw each other often, helped each other, fought with each other, interfered in each other's lives. But friends and neighbors were becoming more important; a friend two doors down the street might be more accessible and frequently more biased in your behalf than a brother or sister two miles away. Some of the old intra-family loyalty had weakened.

In the world outside great events were engulfing people and intruding into the small worlds of family and community. A world war made people realize that they were not totally immune to events across the ocean—a realization they tried to forget once the "war to end all wars" had been won. Government to them was still local government, but never again would Washington be so comfortably remote. The local tax assessor was more real and considerably more important, but the Federal income tax had become a lasting reminder of a more distant power.

More important, industrialization and new technology were changing the conditions of everyday life. The automobile broke the physical isolation of farms and towns; a trip to the nearest city meant a day of shopping, not a major undertaking; visits to friends in another town did not need to be carefully planned all-day events. People began to travel to places several hundred miles away. Vacations became popular. As children grew up, they were no longer tied to family outings, church socials, and their own small group; in a car they could escape the eyes of parents and neighbors and range farther afield, meeting other young people unknown to their families. Parental control weakened, and people were alarmed. Who knew what a boy and girl might be doing, parked on a lonely road alone?

Sex, which had always been trouble enough, was the source of new dangers. It didn't matter so much for boys, although they had no sexual carte blanche, but a girl had more opportunities to become pregnant—which meant "ruining her life" and "disgracing her family," for virginity still had moral and economic value. And young people tried other kinds of experiments: Prohibition, for one thing, made drinking an exciting game. As the 1920's moved on, both girls and boys drank at parties, and on dates in darkened cars. Fashions changed, and short skirts and short hair for girls shocked older people. Stockings were rolled up to leave the knees bare, and a few girls even took to wearing flowing pajama pants. It all added up to a new freedom for youth, new interests and excitement which took them away from family, community, and tradition.

With more new jobs and a greater demand for new

skills, education became more important. Girls as well as boys began to go to college in increasing numbers, and they all came home with strange new ideas. They had never heard about Darwin's theory of evolution in the local high school, where the literal accuracy of Genesis was not usually questioned. They talked about new theories of psychology and discussed writers with strange and often foreign names. They even talked about the need for tolerance, saying that other cultures and other ways of life had a right to be heard, respected, and understood. They were interested in jobs and work that had no roots in the family past, no comforting familiarity with their parents' experience. These young people had gone away to college; worse, they were now planning to go away to work and live. The opportunities of the small town were limited, and they were heading for the cities.

But even for the stay-at-homes, the changes were fast and deep. New jobs and businesses appeared, in gas stations, car showrooms, garages, movie houses, electrical appliance stores. Answers to the question, "What are you going to be when you grow up?" ranged in ever-widening areas. The question was asked of girls as well as boys, although their choices were expected to be more limited and the range of time confined to the period before marriage, for it was still assumed that after their initial fling of independence girls would, like their mothers, return to home and family with no thought of leaving.

Radio and movies brought the outside world into towns and homes. Before, people had largely created their own amusements, and except for the rare traveling show or a week of summer Chautauqua, not much entertainment from the outside reached them. But now the glamour of Hollywood dazzled young and old alike. People wept over the trials of Mary Pickford, thrilled at the adventures of Douglas Fairbanks, laughed at the antics of Laurel and Hardy. They listened to soap operas on the radio, sat up half the night tuning in to distant cities and boasted next day that they had gotten Detroit and Chicago and New York and sometimes even Cuba. They became spectators of a world they had not dreamed existed, and the faces and voices of people they would never meet became as familiar as those of their next-door neighbors.

For people who were parents in those years, the world they had grown up in already seemed remote. Time had telescoped. Parents were often worried and sometimes alarmed; grandparents were confused and frequently shocked. Yet the basic values and structure of the family seemed sound and enduring. To be sure young people talked about "living their own lives," and some people were beginning to say that it was better for young couples to move away from their families and be independent: "They have to leave to stand on their own feet." Still the assumption was they would not veer far from the precepts of the past—even if one did begin now and then to know people who had been divorced.

But before people could catch their breath and begin to understand these changes in their lives, the depression descended like a smothering fog. The blithe faith in the spiral of progress and prosperity was shattered by bread lines, welfare, foreclosures, and repossessions. A stock market that had seemed a permanent Santa Claus turned into a ghost. Local government was helpless to meet people's needs, so for the first time they turned to the Federal government for help with personal needs.

Generations again moved in with each other to save money, and family obligations became urgent and often onerous. Most people did not find it a happy experience, for the order of the old structure was no longer there;

individuals were no longer accustomed to the inevitable conflicts and compromises, the loss of freedom and independence. Children struggled with the confusion of conflicting demands and differing perspectives. No one expected the Depression to last, so there was no incentive to find enduring new ways to adapt to it. Young people escaped when they could, some of them turning to radical new ideas that sought in greater change the fulfillment of ancient dreams. And the Depression dragged on, leaving an indelible imprint on those who experienced it.

A second World War shattered the illusions of enduring peace, of a world done with war. The attack on Pearl Harbor destroyed forever the confident faith in the immunity of America from invasion. Now people scattered from one coast to another, or went across oceans to lands that had sometimes been not even dots on a map to them. They flooded into the armed services and the war industries, or into cities or new towns where everyone was a stranger. Women went to war, worked in factories, or learned skills once the unchallenged domain of men. Marriages were contracted between people who were little more than strangers—marriages that crossed religious lines, cultural, social, and economic lines.

In those four years of war the American family was plunged headlong into a way of life that negated many of the most crucial standards and values by which it had lived. Generations were separated physically and even more by experience, ideas, and perspectives. Parental control was clear only with young children. Community controls were of small import when people were strangers, with no thought of remaining in a given town. Standards of sexual morality, the permanence of marriage, responsibility for children, commitment to the family group and family continuity, the interweaving of family and religion, the authority of elders—all were weakened. Even more devastating, the structure that had integrated all these component parts into a pattern of living had lost the connections that made integration possible and the purpose that gave it power.

When the war ended the family had changed irremediably. Mobility had become a way of life. Relatives were separated with no thought of future reunion. Divorce became common. Children, now economic liabilities, grew up in a world where the areas of human activity were rigorously separated: work from play, education by book from education by life, community from family, religion from just about everything else. And people were separated too.

Men worked at ever greater distances from their home and family; from morning till evening they disappeared into another world. Women sought their own activities and developed their own skills; they no longer assumed that even with marriage and children they would remain at home. As children grew older they sought individuality and self-expression outside the family; with increasing education, they sought careers unrelated to the responsibilities of home and children.

The new generation of parents had been taught the old standards and values, but they had grown up in a world that could not enforce them. As children they had known the Depression, and their memories of family interdependence were not for the most part happy ones. They might still believe in mutual obligations, but they were wary that such obligations should limit their scope to an ever-narrowing family group. They might still believe in responsibility and self-reliance, but these were increasingly related to a world of work outside the family. Thrift and planning wavered under a new hedonism that glorified the immediate, not the distant, future.

Work lost its status as intrinsic virtue and became the servant of increasingly fierce competition. Education was the new mystique; the door to success and riches, the solution to new complexities and problems. Specialization came into its own.

There were great shifts in population as families flocked to the suburbs, escaping the cities that had been the focus of their dreams a generation before. New towns sprang up with no roots in the past, and older ones changed beyond recognition. With fathers absent more and more, responsibility for children fell ever more heavily upon mothers isolated from all the traditional supports of family and community. They became the frantic "Is-what-I'm-doing-right?" parents, the anxious devotees of new theories and experts, the weary sharers of confusion with neighbors who moved, with groups that formed and faded and reformed.

More and more children were responsibilities without specific roles in the family. They too sought activities and interests in the outside world: the organization children. Their family obligations increasingly consisted of fulfilling their parents' expectations of them in that outside world—but these expectations involved individual achievements, not the personal reciprocal responsibilities of the old family. Not a few parents began to look forward to the day when their children would be independent.

The products of affluence increased beyond the most ambitious dreams of the previous generation. Technology and science were the new religion, speed the new commandment, and change, not stability, the supreme value. Television brought new stimulation that affected everyone from the very young to the very old; it had the potential to bring also some measure of understanding, but its common denominator was the commercial. Success came ever earlier, and youth became the test of standards, the criterion of values, the supreme symbol of the exciting New World with its limitless opportunities, and expanding freedoms. New standards and new conformities reflected the new affluence, with its emphasis on individual independence, material rewards, self-development and self-interest.

The old standards and values weakened without the context which had incorporated them and the controls which had enforced them. Parental authority was diminished, not only by their children's increasing involvement with interests outside the home, but also by their own uncertainty and confusion. Women particularly found their roles difficult, as old roles clashed with new ideas, ambitions, and opportunities. The strength of the family was eroded as continuity was lost and separation of the generations became the rule.

Now a generation is coming to maturity that remembers nothing of the old world or the great events that shook it apart. Its values sound meaningless in a structure that did not evolve them and is not designed to further them. The idea of responsibility to the past, to family continuity, has small impact upon people whose own past flickers and changes before their eyes and whose future is problematic. Economic and social responsibility for an older generation rests increasingly with the government or with organizations; the emotional ties that might have mitigated the impersonal indifference of these entities have never grown. Interdependence within the family is barely possible without a common core. Independence and self-reliance have become less virtues than necessities in a society impatient with obligation.

That old lady in her eighties has seen it all. She grew up in a world that seemed intact and enduring. As a young woman she knew the excitement and wonder of the new marvels of technology: she saw the first cars, the first airplanes, the first radios; she remembers when automobiles frightened horses, when roads were unpaved, when people ran outside to watch a plane fly over. She remembers the years of war with sugar shortages and hoarding in 1918, and ration stamps and no new cars and saving bacon grease in 1942. She remembers the day the atomic bomb ended one kind of world and began another. She has lived to see the years when one new marvel treads on the heels of another, and change has become not an orderly process but a kaleidoscope of confusion. She has lived to see change itself become the enduring way of life.

In her lifetime she has seen the family lose its power and much of its purpose. When she was young, she could still take it for granted that her family's interests and her own were closely bound together. She could still assume that her family had a right to intervene even in her choice of a husband. She would not assume that her granddaughter's marriage involved any rights of hers beyond an invitation to the wedding, nor would it have been greatly different with her own children.

Her children, now grandparents themselves, remember some of the old world. Its values are still strong for them, its perspectives a part of their thinking. Though they have been wrenched from its context, they have not lost touch with it. Their children are the first generation to know only a residue of the past, to live with the absence of continuity and commitment, to know the failure of structure. They live with the price of that failure: the confusion, disorder, and emptiness called alienation.

12

CAN THE FAMILY SURVIVE?

Some people believe that the family, as a vital human institution, is finished. Its power gone, it will slowly or speedily deteriorate into another historical dust heap. Others believe it will transform itself into a totally different kind of institution; still others believe it may renew itself and fulfill its ancient functions with new meaning and strength.

It is impossible to imagine what a society without family would be like. The idea seems better adapted to bees or ants than to people. Well-regulated automatons running the machines of an Orwellian world might be the outcome. The children's institutions that raised children from infancy in great, impersonal groups showed how to develop, with a minimum of expense and effort, not so much people as shells of people. If children are to grow up without strong personal attachments, without a consistent structure of discipline, the result is likely to be an inner emptiness for them and increasing violence for society.

Those who foresee great change in family structure observe correctly that we are already traveling in the direction of a peer-group society. People associate with their own age groups and regard other groups with a strange mixture of suspicion and hopeful fantasy or, as with the very old and the very young, don't regard them much at all. The young congregate in communes, turning to each other for advice, help, support. The power of the peer group has turned schools into fields of conflict; more basic, it has challenged the premise of parental authority and the authority of those institutions that depended on it.

There is a current fantasy that the breakdown of such authority will somehow, in time, produce a society of brotherly love. People will fulfill their needs and potentials, which by some new alchemy will not clash but will merge into a peaceful amalgam, with mutual personal concern and a new freedom for everyone. We might well all work to hasten the coming of such a society! Unfortunately neither history nor our knowledge of human beings offers much substance for this hope. Nothing so far revealed by science or technology has offered much promise of Utopia, unless the biological revolution is to alter the basic nature of human beings—in which case all bets are off anyway.

No society has survived without a system of authority. Democracy has essentially depended on self-discipline, the capacity to use freedom for the common good and to administer authority through law. Democracy's ability to survive and grow depends most of all upon people; and here the family has been and remains a most essential factor. It still holds the power and responsibility for that human foundation which makes self-discipline and concern for others possible. With all its faults and weaknesses it has survived monumental changes, and somehow still manages to bring up millions of children with the capacity to adapt to change and to use it productively. It has survived wars, plagues and every known kind of human calamity. It has survived every kind of government, every variation of culture, every barrage of change, every type of economy. With a record like that the family is a force to be reckoned with, a structure to be respected. Its toughness and resilience have few parallels, and not all man's considerable ingenuity has discovered any satisfactory substitutes.

The family confronts today not the loss of its functions but its greatest and most difficult challenge: the rearing of children to the emotional and intellectual maturity that can use our great powers to build a better society, not to destroy all society. The stakes were not so high in the past, nor the demands so nebulous. The responsibilities of parents were not only defined but to a considerable extent were visible. Now parents cannot be sure what is expected of them, and must depend upon their own inner strength to a degree unimaginable in times when the culture set the rules and social controls had the power of religion and tradition to uphold them.

The family has not lost its importance; it *has* lost its power and direction. It is needed more, not less, because now there is no other structure to fulfill that greatest of all needs, the development of a person. The school may teach a child to read, but it cannot teach him to love. Book knowledge may produce scientific competence, but only life knowledge produces competence in living. Only the family can teach the most basic knowledge there is: how to live. When the family fails, there is no other social institution to fill the vacuum. Even religion, which not only supported family strength but stepped in to compensate for family tragedy and weakness, has lost its old authority, and its closeness to the family is broken into mere pieces of contact. Like the family, religion too seeks a renewal of faith and confidence.

There have been such renewals in history for societies, for institutions, for individuals. Democracy renewing its vitality out of the dead weight of autocracy, Britain planning a new society when survival itself was at stake, Handel composing the "Hallelujah Chorus" out of the depths of despair. The family is not doomed to slide into ever more vitiating weakness and futility; it may instead stand on the threshold of its most important era. Its challenge is not physical survival, as in the past, but emotional survival, the creation not of abundance but of the values to use abundance for a life worth living. By one of history's greatest ironies, such values may be our only chance of physical survival. As John Gardner has pointed out, "Our problem is not to find better values, but rather to be faithful to those we profess." It seems an overwhelming if not impossible challenge, but a great need can generate a great faith. It is the absence of need that destroys the soul.

If society decides that the family is indispensable for the teaching of those values upon which society's survival may depend, the family's importance will grow, will no longer be taken for granted; it will take precedence. That in itself would have a revolutionary impact upon the nature of the family. Imagine what would happen if we devoted to strengthening the family even one quarter of the energy that we devote to strengthening the economy. People would become important as people, not simply as consumers; children would matter for their own sakes, not as means to adult purposes that bear no relation to children's needs. When we see vitally important purpose in the family, we will make it important, and in so doing we may create the greatest revolution of all.

We neither can nor should go back to the old family. The structure of the family, like its purpose, has been changing for a long time. The precise shape it takes will depend on its purpose and on the conditions of life itself. What the family must retain and renew and build upon are the values that create a society worth preserving and fighting for. But certain realities are already clear.

The number of children in a family will be small. Without population control it is unlikely that either the individual or the values evoked by the concept of the individual can survive. Physical survival itself may be jeopardized. Overcrowding, growing enclaves of surplus people for whom society has no need or place, despoiling of the environment—all lead to negation of the individual and to the weakening of human values. Many responsible young people already sharply limit the size of their family and adopt when they want more children. As the large family was once the standard, the small family must now become the model for public approval.

With small families the job of being parents will be intensive but confined to a small time span. When the focus is truly on the importance of children, that time span may become one of the most creative periods in the lives of both parents. With our emphasis on competition and the importance of organized activities and achievements, we have offered little incentive and stimulation to the development of human relationships. Instead of a period of dullness and restriction when women stagnate at home, this time of the raising of children might be a time of growth and satisfaction. Today there are many ways mothers can be relieved from the too great intensity of day-by-day responsibility. For example, in some neighborhoods young mothers have created their own self-help cooperatives, in which one mother cares for a small group of children for a half-day a week, and the responsibility is rotated.

Such developments point to another necessary change: the family's isolation must be broken if family is to survive and give what it is uniquely responsible for giving. It is simply not sensible to ask two people, usually young and inexperienced, to assume important and complex responsibilities without any resources or support. The family never before operated in splendid isolation, and in a time of great confusion it is even more vulnerable. But there is probably no way to increase support of the family and assistance to parents except in the renewal of community. It is unlikely that relatives can again become a power in the family. A community in the true sense, however, might do more to provide roots for people and strength for the family than any other social institution. But the question has to be faced: can community be reborn?

In the last few generations, with the explosion of scientific knowledge and its application in technology, we have concentrated on the goal of materialism. Progress has been defined by it; family and community have served loyally in its advance. It came so fast and offered such lavish gifts that no one could take the time to assess its cost. But only now do the human and environmental costs begin to be visible. Suddenly people want to escape progress; they look for ways to shut out the conflict, violence, and destructiveness that have followed in its wake. Ethnic groups, occupational groups, age groups seek in homogeneity a security that says "within this circle people are safe," and they pay the ancient price of perceiving others as strangers or even enemies. While modern transportation and communications widen horizons, personal communication falters. With unity an ever more urgent necessity for survival, divisiveness grows with fear.

There is a human ecology, and like the ecology of physical environment human actions have unexpected and far-reaching consequences. When we destroyed the unity of family and community, segmenting each into isolated fragments, we ignored the fact that people, like trees, require individual roots for growth. The structure of life no longer left time for growth, and personal roots seemed irrelevant. History lost its meaning for the individual as well as for society, and in the process the importance of childhood was denied. Children are not materialists. They prefer people to things, continuity to change, routine to diversity. How they feel about themselves is more important as a measure of success than what they have, and how they feel about themselves is a reflection of how their parents feel about them. In short, children simply don't fit many of the dominant values of our society.

Now many young people call for the primacy of human concern and correctly assess what its loss must mean for society. They want personal concern and commitment, a reversal of bureaucratic indifference and official callousness. But personal concern, like other human qualities, is grown. It begins with receiving concern from others, moves to mutual concern as a part of mutual need, expands to those familiar and similar— and only with maturity and knowledge encircles the stranger and the alien. Without that maturity, brotherly love is likely to become brotherly need, frustrated and tenuous, containing within it the seeds of its own destruction.

The answer to the possibility of renewal of family and community lies in what we decide is of first importance. More than anything it requires a change in attitude and priorities. That is a new challenge; no such choice was necessary for family and community in the past. Then behavior, not feelings as such, was the focus; the emotional welfare of the individual was not ignored, but it was assumed to be part of the general welfare. The new challenge of family and community is to find a new balance, a new unity between the two.

The precise form of community, as of family, depends upon its goals. If it seeks to contribute to unity, it will not opt for homogeneity in a heterogeneous society. And that also represents a new challenge. If community seeks to become once again an agent of social control, it must formulate essential standards. It cannot turn its back upon child neglect and child abuse with the rationalization that they are the concern only of the family or of officialdom. It must once again demand from the family specific obligations and provide an environment which encourages their fulfillment. If a community is to meet personal needs, it must become a personal community with a place for its members of all ages, economic levels, races, and religions, a place where people are needed and wanted. In other words, a living community must become again a place where people belong.

That is a task immeasurably more difficult now than in the past. It requires a core of permanence in a structure of flexibility. Yet that has been achieved in the past. The Jews kept religion and family intact during two thousand years of change, adaptation, and relentless pressures, for they knew it was their only means of survival. And it may be the only means for modern society. Unlike the Jews, however, modern society in general lacks a common faith, but it does have a tradition of humanist values growing out of the great Judeo-Christian heritage. Even when those values are honored more in words than in action, they remain constant, because basic human needs remain constant. As we are learning through bitter experience, no amount of affluence answers them.

Certain things must change if community is to meet those needs. First among them is mobility. Families have been moved around at the instigation of business and industry without regard for family cohesion. It is simply assumed that a man's career and his family's welfare are, if not synonymous, essentially in harmony. The family's relationships with him, with friends, with community can be broken abruptly and with impunity and reestablished hundreds or thousands of miles away with new friends and a new community, if not with new relatives.

The whole process is neatly summed up by a moving company's TV commercial. A man's lonely footsteps echo through an empty house while a mellifluous male voice describes the tree the children used to climb, the chip in the wall where a tricycle came to grief, the mound in the garden where a favorite kitten is buried. Then the voice turns cheerful: in a week or two the family will be settled in a new house, and everyone will be making new friends, enjoying new activities or the same old ones in new settings.

For a time it seemed to be just about that simple. People moved, sometimes by the thousands, to better climates, more exciting areas, more diverse opportunities. There was a heady feeling of freedom about it all, a quality of adventure and stimulation, particularly for people recently rooted in the monotony of one setting. Now the cost of rootlessness has outweighed the freedom, and the excitement has dissipated in anxiety. Mobility, with its necessary disruption of continuing relationships, ends by starving them into superficiality, and friendship becomes little more than acquaintance. Experiences shared with a succession of unconnected people become more impressions than lasting parts of a life pattern. They cannot have the same impact upon a person, because they too tend to be isolated fragments, without the connections to give them meaning.

Community involvement alters in nature when there is no shared past and no solid commitment to the future. It lacks urgency, and personal investment has to be less personal. In a sense people lose their past because there is no one to share it with them. As one woman said, "When my mother died, I suddenly realized I had lost the last person who knew me as a little girl. I was an only child and, because my family had moved a good deal, my childhood friends were scattered. In any case they had only shared pieces of my past. I felt as if I had lost a part of myself because there was no one left who had known me as I was." People have lost the feeling of belonging, not because they wanted or planned to, but because they took it for granted. It is possible that without personal belonging there is no bridge to belonging to larger entities, that the unity of a nation is weakened when the continuity of community and family belonging are destroyed.

One hopeful sign is that mobility is losing its glamour. People are beginning to move less from desire for change, and to resent the necessity. Some men are objecting to industry-imposed transfers and are refusing to move, even when a move means a promotion and more money. Some families are by preference living in smaller communities where there is less opportunity for economic advancement but more opportunity for family life. Here and there people move completely away from the competition and struggle and settle permanently in a quiet retreat where family members have time for each other and opportunity for common interests. Again, they usually sacrifice economic to human advantage.

Even more hopeful is the growing social approval that accompanies such moves. Where before such people would have been labeled peculiar if not downright stupid, they are now regarded almost with envy. Another TV commercial glorifies the man intelligent enough to get out of the rat race. A TV serial praises the girl who gives up a good job out of town to stay with her family. (To be sure, it is a woman, not a man, who makes the decision, and at that she is a sister who has the role of mother without actually being the mother.) The signs may still be small ones, but they are there.

Some people believe that the great business and industrial organizations will absorb the family and in effect become its continuity, its roots. Certain companies almost do that now. One has made a great success by literally becoming the life and security of its employees' families. One young man said rather bitterly, "The company will become your family. Dear old Mother Mutual will look after everything and you'll spend your whole life with her." One can only hope profoundly that this modern feudalism does not represent any trend of the future. The business organization will inevitably use the family for its own ends and shape it to its own needs; some have already subverted family integrity in the service of their own purposes. Even the less dangerous idea that the community of the future will be formed on professional and occupational identities can only set up false barriers to the vital community in which family as a unique structure can flourish.

As industry moves out of metropolitan centers, new towns grow up. People live closer to their work, and fathers can have more time at home. There is opportunity for more space, for closer relationships, for more shared activities. Whether these represent trends more favorable to a rebirth of community depends upon what people really want. Continuing involvement, a greater sense of belonging, require different kinds of compromises than people are now accustomed to. It means, for example, facing inevitable problems and unpleasantness and working them out rather than escaping them. That was easier in the communities of the past because in those communities, by and large, people had no choice. They worked out a good many problems that they would probably have preferred to escape if preference had been part of the picture. That was true for families too. When change is difficult and choice limited, people must develop qualities that work at solving the problems. For some time now they haven't had to do that, so frustration has become an evil to be abolished, not a challenge to be met. If the reward of continuity and struggle is a renewal of human values, its price is certainly frustration endured and transformed.

If, as seems probable, the family is to become an ever smaller unit, its responsibility limited in time, women must have educational opportunities open to them at various stages of their lives. They should be able to go to school to develop new skills and interests without incurring penalties because they spent years bringing up children. That experience has great value, and many fields of work can use talented mothers to great advantage. Such talents have not recently been valued and rewarded, and the experience of women as mothers has not often been regarded as relevant to careers. Yet a successful mother must develop qualities of concern, judgment, and understanding that are the scarcest and most desperately needed qualities of all. She must develop skills of organization and integration that can be used in many areas of human affairs. We have looked on motherhood as a hiatus in the continuity of building a career, not as a valuable and enriching part of it. There are women, as there are men, with a talent for helping human beings, but it is a talent not yet highly regarded or rewarded by our society.

Since women will certainly continue to work in increasing numbers, it becomes essential that their families should be neither a penalty nor a side-interest. There is no more rigorous or demanding education than that required of a good mother, and it should command the respect that society reserves for its best.

Whatever the structure of the family, it needs more people. At this point there are either too many emotional eggs in one basket or, as is increasingly true, not enough invested in any one place. There are plenty of groups and plenty of people; the scarcity lies in the person-to-person relationships that grow personal responsibility and personal concern. This was the special gift of the extended family: it provided the opportunity for children to know adults other than their parents intimately, within the structure of the kinship system. It is impossible to predict how similar results might be achieved in a society in transition. Possibly over time the family may move away from its small nucleus of parents and children into some wider form of kinship system.

Some communes seem to be moving in that direction

now. Their great weakness, of course, is that they lack a unifying principle. Kinship and religion have been the only two forces capable of welding a communal group into any degree of continuity and mutual responsibility, and both have institutionalized a structure of authority and protection. It is highly improbable that, in the absence of such a structure, personal commitments can produce more than a transient phenomenon. The peer group is essentially more divisive than unitary, and when it includes children in its scope, it introduces a new source of conflict, whatever its idealized dreams. Its attempt to achieve cohesion by the old in-group-against-the-rest-of-the-world method is in itself regressive and more productive of future dissention than of continuity. A new family structure must have a more realistic foundation than the new communes have, and it must be a functioning part of society, not a refuge from it.

Yet monogamy is losing its power, and with it a whole code of family morality. Originally a structure for the protection of women and children, monogamy is now attacked by women as well as men. The sexual revolution, whatever its present impact upon behavior, substitutes personal feeling for the old standard of continuing commitment. Yet personal feeling without institutionalized structure and controls leads to chaos; in the absence of a level of personal maturity not yet generally visible, it is no basis for the kind of social organization that would be a bulwark against chaos.

Modern trends in marriage may be moving in the direction of the old Roman idea of two kinds of marriage. With modern contraception and the liberalization of abortion laws, there could well be legalized a kind of marriage that made no commitment of permanence, ended financial obligations upon its dissolution, and would endure only as long as the individuals involved determined. It would reduce some of the conflict and bitterness in modern marriage because by its nature it would limit expectations. So long as it lasted it would have legal status, thus simplifying some of the complications of no-marriage relationships.

A second kind of marriage would be marriage in the traditional sense, and would mean children. Here the interests of the children could take precedence. The commitment of the marriage, with its accompanying obligations, would focus on the children's needs; and the commitment could be far more decisive—at least while the children are growing up—because it would require conscious decision and choice. Such a commitment might go a long way toward clarifying the conflict between the rights of children and the rights of parents. It would renew the important bond between rights and obligations. At present we neither release people for a marriage free of on-going responsibility nor demand from them the serious commitment that the protection of children requires.

The conflicts arising from a confusion of expectations and from a concept of self-expression divorced from obligation to the helpless young could be reduced by a definitive division of marriage itself. Free marriage could be turned into committed marriage, and the state could formally sanction each by its own appropriate means. Whatever the complications of such a system, it could serve to return dignity and importance to the family without denigrating those who choose different goals and seek a different kind of personal freedom. It might, because it would demand a definite decision, give new strength to the tie between independence and responsibility. Choice in serious life decisions is not a cafeteria but a first step in a long chain of consequences.

While none of this would increase the size of family,

it might well strengthen the importance of parenthood, and it might, over time, revitalize some kinship ties. By giving new importance to family, it might enable family as structure to reach out and incorporate new sources of strength. Thus community, as it did in the past, might come to compensate in some degree for the loss of the extended family.

Whatever structure the family evolves into, it must, if it is to survive, answer certain basic human needs. It must protect the young and civilize them—a very complicated process. It is a personal, not a group process, and so long as human beings learn by identification, children will require close and continuing contact with parents or parent substitutes. The family must provide personal security and refuge to its members, including its growing body of older people. It is the family that has taught loyalty, discipline, responsibility, and obligation, qualities that can be carried from the family to the larger society. They are all qualities essential in a democracy; they are also qualities essential for a complete personality.

The family is the last bastion against mass society. The emptiness, impersonality, and destructiveness of a mass society producing mass man and mass woman not only threaten survival but raise the question of whether such a society deserves to survive. The individual cannot withstand the onslaught of a mass society, and without social institutions that protect and nurture him as a person, he must become submerged in anonymity. Not even his sins are important except as they become monstrous. Modern society posts its warnings. Change that has no time for integration of the new and transformation of the old becomes chaos. Progress loses its meaning and becomes senseless novelty: speed without destination.

Destructiveness becomes irrational and venomous. Mass society devoid of personal compassion becomes mass psychosis.

None of this is inevitable unless one is to assume that human beings are incapable of a personal development that surpasses adolescence, that their intelligence may apply to everything but themselves. We have the power to make a better life for people than the world has ever known. The result depends on the values we choose and the price we are willing to pay for them. In Plutarch's words—which is to come first, our feet or our shoes?

Catalog

If you are interested in a list of fine Paperback
books, covering a wide range of subjects
and interests, send your name and address,
requesting your free catalog, to:

McGraw-Hill Paperbacks
1221 Avenue of Americas
New York, N.Y. 10020